DEO GRATIAS

*Cover: Detail of stained-glass window by Joseph Benoit at
St. Matthew's Church depicting Church and Convent
(Photograph by Diane Moore)*

View of Maison Saint-Louis and Weather Tower, early 1900s
(Courtesy of Arthur Blundell)

Deo Gratias

*A History of the
French Catholic Church
in Jersey: 1790-2007*

Diane Moore

Published in 2007 by
Les Amitiés Franco-Britanniques de Jersey
Maison de la Normandie et de la Manche
71 Halkett Place
St. Helier
Jersey   JE2 4WG

Origination by
Seaflower Books
Jersey

Printed by Cromwell Press
Trowbridge, Wiltshire

ISBN 978-0-9556606-0-3

Contents

*St. Ouen and St. John; The De La Salle Brothers; The Oblates move
East; St. Joseph's, Grouville; Expansion in St. Thomas' Parish;
Père Donat Michaux; Laying the Foundation Stone at St. Thomas';
Four Years Later; The Little Sisters of the Poor; Debts, Death and
Renewal; The Limes; End of a Century.*

III   A New Century: 1900-1939

IV   War

V   A Changing World: 1945-2007

Yvonne Benest: March 25th 1908 – February 28th 2003

Foreword

This book is dedicated to the memory of Yvonne Benest, in recognition of her devout Catholic faith, and of her loyal support of *Les Amitiés Franco-Britanniques de Jersey*, of which she was a member for over fifty years. She was born in St. Servan in Britanny, and, after a happy and privileged childhood, she trained as a nurse with La Croix Rouge Française, staying at her post as a theatre nurse during the terrible bombardment of St. Malo towards the end of World War Two. She moved to Jersey and in 1953 was married to Ernest Benest. Their happy marriage came to a premature end when Ernest died in 1968, but Yvonne continued to charm all those around her with her vitality and boundless energy. She thoroughly enjoyed attending meetings of *Les Amitiés*, and it was her wish that, upon her death, they should receive a bequest, to use as the Committee saw fit. With Yvonne's deeply held religious beliefs in mind, the members decided to commission research into the history of the French Catholic Church in Jersey – from its reintroduction after the French Revolution, when British attitudes to "Rome" became more tolerant. Jersey has willingly accepted émigrés over the centuries, providing them with a safe haven during times of persecution, whether religious or political, and the result of the commissioned research is this book. It will, I am sure, be of great value to everyone with an interest in a page of history that, but for Yvonne, might not have been researched during the lifetime of the author's witnesses: the work is, therefore, an invaluable record, and it will be treasured by the many people who knew her. For Yvonne Benest's life, and for Diane Moore's book, *Deo Gratias*.

Robin Pallot
Honorary French Consul
October 2007

Acknowledgements

I would like to thank everyone who helped me during this project. Above all, special thanks go to Robin Pallot and the *Amitiés Franco-Britanniques* for asking me to undertake this study in the first place. It has turned out to be a great journey of discovery. I am also indebted to the Jersey Library, Jersey Archive, Jersey Museum, La Société Jersiaise, the *Jersey Evening Post*, the Catholic Church in Jersey, the Archives of the Frères de l'Instruction Chrétienne de Ploërmel, the OMI Libraries and Archives in Pontmain, Rome and Dublin, the Carmel de Saint-Pair, the Town Hall of Saint-Mars-la-Réorthe and various other establishments. I would like to thank my father Don Barnett and my daughter Marianne Enget for their encouragement and patience; and I feel privileged to have had the enthusiastic support of my mother Jeanne Moore, who sadly passed away on July 20th 2007 and did not see the finished book. I am indebted to Sister Peter, Pat Lucas and Jean Andersson for proofreading my texts, and I would also like to mention the following to whom I am grateful in many ways – for lending me their old photographs for this book or for giving me individual help and advice.

Peter Abrams, Yvon Beaudoin O.M.I., Arthur Blundell, Edouard Bosquet, Tom Bowen, Richard Brocken, Barbara Cabot, Andrew Colter, Pierrette Corsane, Pierre Court O.M.I., Alasdair Crosby, Guy Dixon, Bernard Durand, Michael and Pat Edmunds, Andrée and John Etienne, Canon Nicholas France, Deanna Greene, Frère Vincent Guillerm, Jan Hadley, David Hick, Bernard Holley, Michael Hughes O.M.I., Sister Ida, Vincent Igoa O.M.I., Marcia Jameson, Carol Jordi, Jack and Barbara Jouanny, Phil and Karen Le Cornu, Gérard and Roma Lecrivain, Elspeth Legg, Aurélie Leroy, Rev. Iain MacFirbhisigh, Tom McCabe O.M.I., Sister Marie-Louise, Heather Morton, Eileen and

ACKNOWLEDGEMENTS

Paul Nicolle, Val Nelson, Brother Richard Oliver, Sister Pascaline, Anthony Pezet, Sister Phyllis, Frère Yves Pichon, Frère Joseph Pinel, Cecil Rebours, Mary Renouf, Brenda Ross, Edward Sallis, John Sankey, Phyllis Simon, Michael Vautier, Jackie Watson, Jennifer Ward, Rev. Tony Ward, Tony Weeks.

If I have omitted anyone, *mea culpa*!

Diane Moore
October 2007

Introduction

The aims of this book are to present a dynamic and living testimony to all those French Catholics who came to Jersey since the French Revolution, seeking religious renewal, peace and safety in this Island. A testimony to the legacy they have left us, now such a precious part of our Island heritage.

I start my story during the French Revolution, charting the resurgence of a faith previously banished from Jersey. I do not aspire to delve into the Reformation in Jersey, nor do I seek to study in detail the gamut of internal disputes which coloured Jersey's history between the Reformation and the re-establishment of a Catholic Church on the Island. Various eminent historians have already covered these aspects, not least the late G.R.Balleine in his monumental *History of Jersey*.[1] However, frequent voyages back in time will be made during the course of this work, which will aim to chart the renaissance of a Roman Catholic French community in Jersey, how it re-established itself, re-invented itself, and evolved from that historic moment in the early 1790s to the French Catholic community Jersey carved for itself during the years to follow.

Needless to say, a study of the Catholic Faith in Jersey from 1790 to the present day could fill many tomes of writing and keep doctoral students busy for decades; it has therefore been necessary for me to limit myself, and adhere to the wishes of Madame Yvonne Benest to whose memory this book is dedicated. Focusing principally on the history of French Catholicism in Jersey, this work does not in any way overlook the major importance of Anglo-Irish Catholicism in the Island, and in more recent years, the impact of the Portuguese and Polish communities. These vast areas, I am sure, will become the subject of further research in the years to come.

I am immensely grateful to those whose memories have made it possible to chart the history of French Catholicism on the Island. I certainly feel I have written a history book, but one which also captures history in movement, and I hope that the numerous illustrations and photographs I have chosen for this publication will shed as much light on the topic as the areas of in-depth documentary research which was necessary to create the work. Finally, I sincerely hope that this book will remind us how important it is to embrace our heritage and to protect the tangible reminders we have of the past which contributed so significantly to shape our future. The French priests may have left Jersey, but the powerful legacy they left us in the realm of education, knowledge, architecture and faith should never be forgotten.

I

The Return of Catholicism

1790-1880

1   Radical Changes

The French Revolution

1789. France was in turmoil, turmoil so deep and complex that debate still rages amongst historians today as to the precise socio-political and economic causes of the French Revolution. However, it was clear that the rigid social structure of French society during the *Ancien Régime*[1] was collapsing.

For centuries French society had been divided into three *Etats*, which for convenience and understanding we shall refer to as States:[2] The First State consisted of the clergy and the Second State the nobility. Together, these two States accounted for approximately 500,000 French inhabitants. At the bottom of this hierarchy was the vast Third State which comprised mainly of the bourgeoisie and peasants, about 25 million people. This social structure was based on custom and tradition, but more importantly, it was also based on huge inequalities which were sanctioned by the force of law. The First and Second States did not pay taxes, the third did.

However, radical changes were tainting this old order. France was in a state of financial crisis – huge debts were sustained as a result of the various wars of the eighteenth Century and by the reigning King Louis XVI's massive spending; in addition, the country's taxation system was totally inequitable. Coupled with this was the rising spirit of the Enlightenment *philosophes* – writers such as Diderot,[3] Voltaire[4] and Jean-Jacques Rousseau[5] had fuelled the minds of French intellectuals, and whilst they did not actually advocate revolution in any of their writings, they did awaken a feeling of resentment of (a) the financial privileges of the Clergy – the first of the three States – and (b) the power of the Church's rituals to instill superstitious fear in people's minds. Academic and literate Frenchmen were becoming intellectually critical of this state of affairs and, following the principles of the Enlightenment *philosophes,* began to advocate the use of reasoning and criticism. They knew that questioning accepted ideas and conventions could effect change: a change in ethics, a change in knowledge and education, a change in human conditions.

From the outset, the Church was privileged. The French Catholic Church maintained a wide scope of powers – it literally constituted a state within a state and it had sustained this position for more than 800 years. The clergy was divided into the lower and upper clergy. Members of the lower clergy were usually humble, poorly-paid and overworked village priests. As a group, they resented the wealth and arrogance of the upper clergy. The bishops and abbots filled the ranks of the upper clergy, and many of these regarded their office as a way of securing a larger income and the landed property that went with it. Some of the upper clergy sold their offices to subordinates, kept the revenue, and lived in Paris or at the seat of royal government at Versailles. They also owned 10-15% of all the land in France. This land, of course, was all held tax-free.

Hoping to avert a financial disaster, Louis XVI was forced to call the three States to Versailles for a general meeting and election, the first of its kind since 1614, the aim being to obtain the assembly's consent to a general fiscal reform. This took place on May 5th 1789. However, as the much larger Third State objected to a voting system which would deprive them of a proportionate vote, they defiantly declared themselves the National Assembly on June 17th. A few minor nobles and members of the clergy joined them. Within a week, the king was forced to legalise this.

Parisians mobilised, and on July 14th stormed the Bastille fortress. Louis XVI was obliged to accept the tricolour cockade of the Revolution from the newly formed municipal government. This first outbreak of violence marked the entry of the popular classes into the Revolution. Peasants looted and burned castles and mansions, destroying all records of feudal dues: this initial period of violence is known as *La Grande Peur* – the great fear.

On August 4th, the nobles and clergy in the Assembly, driven partly by fear and partly by an outburst of idealism, relinquished their privileges, abolishing in one night the feudal structure of France. Shortly afterward, the Assembly adopted the *Déclaration des Droits de l'Homme et du Citoyen,*[6] one of the fundamental documents of the French Revolution which defined a set of individual rights and collective rights of all of the States as one.

The Assembly's anticlerical measures had the gravest consequence for many clergy members: Church lands were nationalized (1789), religious orders suppressed (1790), and the clergy required (July, 1790) to swear to adhere to the state-controlled *Constitution civile du clergé.*[7] Only a bare majority (52%) of all priests took the oath, many wishing to adhere to papal sovereignty; disturbances broke out, especially in western France, and Louis XVI, though forced to assent, was roused to action. Numerous princes and nobles had already fled abroad as *émigrés.* Louis decided to join them to obtain foreign aid to restore his authority. The flight (June 20-21, 1791) was halted at Varennes, and the king and queen were brought back in humiliation. Louis accepted the constitution.

The Religious *Emigrés*

In eighteenth-century France, ninety-five percent of the population were adherents to the Roman Catholic faith, and under the *Ancien Régime*, the authority of the Church was institutionalized in its status as the First State, foremost among the three States. As we have seen, the power of the Roman Catholic Church came from many sources, and no citizen in France could live his or her life without the involvement of the Roman Catholic Church.

Yet whilst history books have painted a clear picture of the tax-exempt lifestyle of many of the wealthier, fear-instilling institutions within the Church, the very fact that only 52% of the clergy actually swore the oath to adhere to the state-controlled *Civil Constitution of the Clergy* points to the fact that a large number of priests and men of the cloth did not. This begs a question – why, when faced with the current violence, uncertainty and radical change in France, coupled with the imminent escalation in the bloodshed, leading to what would become *La Terreur,* did thousands of clergymen and women staunchly adhere to their own beliefs and seek exile or risk death for the sake of their faith? One straightforward answer is that a large number of these men and women simply refused to take orders from anyone other than the Pope, and as the Pope denounced the Constitution, this resulted in a split in the French Catholic Church. Those who accepted the new order were known as the constitutional clergy, and those who obeyed the Pope, the refractory priests or "non-jurors". Many of these, now banished from their places of worship, were not amongst the wealthy minority who had exploited faith to increase their power, but were from more humble backgrounds; others, bishops included, preferred to lose status than sign an oath they felt would be an act of betrayal to Rome. Whatever rank they came from, they quite simply refused to accept a new regime which was beginning to spiral out of control and which was disillusioning many Frenchmen and foreigners alike by its sheer scale of barbarity. The new government viewed any non-conformist sector of the Church as being at the heart of the Counter-Revolution, and draconian measures were being taken to dechristianise France. These measures developed into *La Terreur*.

Between 1792 and 1794, thousands of priests and nuns were deported or forced into exile to flee the horrific massacres and persecutions which became widespread throughout France. The country's infrastructure had become so anti-clerical that under the new Republican system Sundays had been abolished, divorce was legalised and the old Gregorian calendar replaced with a new Republican Calendar.[8] Many foreign countries, which at first had shown some sympathy for the Revolution's goals, were horrified by the scope of the violence and persecution of the clergy.

The *émigrés* were deported to countries which could harbour them safely. The Channel Islands, by their geographical location and historical and linguistic ties with France, were an obvious choice for those men and women of the cloth who were fleeing Western France.

Turmoil in Jersey

However, the Channel Islands were not without their own socio-political turmoil, and whilst the *émigrés* and aristocrats began to pour onto our shores, Jersey was still smarting from two recent French attempts to capture the Island.[9] Geographically, the Channel Islands were the frontline position in the war against France, and as France technically was the enemy, this put Jersey in a position of significant physical and diplomatic tension. It also explains why there was a degree of suspicion and dissatisfaction within the local community regarding the arrival of French refugees.

On the domestic front, Jersey was also having its internal battles and mini-revolutions: during the course of the century the Island's autocratic bailiffship was under considerable strain. Since November 1750, Charles Lemprière had been the absent Bailiff's Lieutenant, and by all intents and purposes adopted the role of Bailiff. During the following thirty years of his office, Lemprière's manner of governing Jersey reached the stage where many Islanders felt they were living under a quasi-dictatorship. Dissatisfaction and uprisings were inevitable; this led to the emergence of an opposition and the subsequent creation of two political factions. Those who supported Lemprière became known as the Charlots and those who backed Jean Dumaresq, champion of the more liberal, idealistic movement, were initially given the title Jeannots, although they soon became widely known as the Magots.[10]

How these parties related to the arrival of and behaviour towards the French *émigrés* is of significance: in many respects, the Charlots (now led by Charles Lemprière's even more anti-democratic son William Charles) were a one-man show supported by a group of die-hard Jurats. The Magots, on the other hand, were strongly influenced by the thoughts of the French Enlightenment *philosophes*, and were fuelled by the idealism of the latent revolutionary spirit in France, seemingly unaware of the horrific consequences the bloody rebellion would have on the population. In the years leading up to the French Revolution, the Magots' close ally, Mathieu Alexandre, set up the first printing press in the Island, launching the monthly *Magasin de l'Ile de Jersey*. A libellous article soon ended the course of this publication, but it was followed shortly after by the creation of Jersey's first newspaper, *Gazette de l'Ile de Jersey*, again produced by Dumaresq's ally Alexandre. It was through this mouthpiece, which openly welcomed the French Revolution even as late as 1792, that any anti-*émigré* propaganda was spread through the Island.[11]

The *Emigrés* Arrive in Jersey

The first French *émigrés* arrived in Jersey at the beginning of 1790. Most of these were French nobles. By the end of March that year, at least four boatloads of French men and women had reached the Island,

and as the Island's only newspaper, the *Gazette de l'Ile de Jersey* was only too eager to condemn these events knowing that there was no rival publication to riposte their views. However, as it turned out, the majority of Jersey readers were appalled by the *Gazette*'s attitude, and a public outcry ensued. The newspaper, wanting to demonstrate its alleged democratic stance, permitted letters to the Editor, and many of these led to replies in the form of poems, short notes or appeals to the public, often signed anonymously. The *Gazette* was also forced to apologise for its offending remarks, and in the issue of April 10th 1790, had to concede that it did not "have the slightest intention of troubling the hospitality or dampening the welcome that the people of this island are giving the foreigners." The *Gazette* did attempt to condemn the *émigrés* on a few other occasions, and Baron E. de Demuin, in his *Histoire Religieuse de Jersey,*[12] one of the most informative works regarding the history of religion in Jersey, refers to a number of incidents involving hostility to the French. On one particular occasion, shots were fired into a house believed to be full of *émigrés*. As it happened, there was only one French woman living there, and she escaped unscathed. The impression given by Demuin in his book is quite unambiguous: the Jersey Monarchists, chiefly the Charlots, gave the *émigrés* a great deal of support, whilst the Magots, zealously supporting the idealist philosophy fuelling the French Revolution, condemned the French nobles and clergy at more than one point in time.

Over the coming months, members of the French clergy began to flood into Jersey, Bishop Augustin Le Mintier of Tréguier being one of the first – he arrived in St. Helier in March 1791. Conscious of the political tension that the forthcoming influx to the Island could create, and aware that his own arrival had caused a stir in the *Gazette*,[13] he felt a need for diplomacy, and by all accounts paved the way for the refugees' arrival, gaining the support of many Jerseymen and women.

Bishop Le Mintier was closely assisted by two Breton priests, Père Luc Chantrel from St. Malo, and Père Guy Carron from St-Germain in Rennes (who had become a much-loved figure in his district for having helped to open a cotton factory for the poor, and who had preferred to risk his life rather than sign the Constitutional Oath). Boatload upon boatload of exiled clergymen and women reached Jersey's shores, and whilst the constant ferrying of refugees from France also provided Jersey boatmen with brisk if not perilous trade, the sudden twofold increase in St. Helier's population gave cause for concern amongst the locals. Emergency accommodation had to be provided, and an attempt was made to place many of the emigrants into existing shelters in the smaller municipalities of St. Aubin, Gorey, Beaumont and Millbrook. Conditions were tough. In the book, *Banished by the Revolution*, Father Francis P. Isherwood (editor) quotes an eye-witness account of the misery surrounding the conditions of some of the *émigrés*:

> It is impossible to paint a proper picture of the terrible destitution suffered by these virtuous ministers of the Altar. Most of them have no linen, no proper clothes, and no means of buying any. I remember how, when they first arrived in the Island, a large building that had once been a school for poor children was rented for them. They all slept in the one room on mattresses that other refugees, already living in Jersey, had given them.[14]

The sudden doubling of the population of St. Helier did not go unchallenged by those who fiercely opposed their arrival, and a number of incidents were reported. Ultimately, on December 15th 1792, an anonymous supporter of the refugees managed to have a letter published in the *Gazette*. Referring to himself as *"L'Ami des Infortunés"* (The Friend of the Ill-fated), he wrote:

> What are you thinking about, you *Jersiais*, you who have the reputation of being *human*? Take care lest this flattering fame is not tarnished by the cruel behaviour that some rogues are showing towards the unfortunate who seek refuge amongst you.[15]

Chateaubriand

One of the most well-known *émigrés* to set foot in Jersey was the French writer François-René de Chateaubriand.[16] In 1792, he had joined the army of the French Royalist *émigrés*, and was wounded in a major clash with the French Republican Army at Thionville. It was from there that he was brought to Jersey en route to London as an exile. Jersey was the obvious choice, as he already had relatives living here who were able to take care of him. In his *Mémoires d'Outre-Tombe*, (*Memoirs from Beyond the Grave*) published between 1848 and 1850, he refers to his arrival in the Island:

> We set sail, and reached the most westerly point of Jersey. Monsieur de Tilleul, one of my companions, went to my uncle in St Helier. The next day, Monsieur de Bedée came to fetch me in a carriage. We crossed the whole island: although I felt I was at death's door, I was nonetheless enchanted by its hedged fields: but I just talked sheer nonsense, having fallen into a fever.
>
> For four months I hovered between life and death. My uncle, his wife, his son and three daughters took turns beside my bed. I occupied an apartment in one of the houses they had begun to build along the shore: my bedroom windows reached the floor, and beyond the end of my bed I could see the sea. The doctor, Monsieur Delattre, had forbidden them to talk about anything serious with me, and most certainly not politics. Towards the end of January 1793, my uncle entered my room in full mourning, and I trembled, assuming we had lost a member of the family: he informed me of the death of Louis XVI. I was not surprised; I had predicted it. I asked for news of my relatives; my sisters and my wife had returned to Brittany briefly after the September Massacres; they had had a lot of trouble getting out of Paris.[17]

Amongst the written sources on the subject of the *émigrés* who spent time in Jersey, some of them list the names of individual refugees; one of these works is a volume by Régis-Marie-Joseph de l'Estourbeillon de la Garnache[18] who compiled a complete register of the approximate 3,200 priests who stayed in Jersey (as well as other French *émigrés*); other authors include Abbé Amédée Guillotin de Corson[19] and, as mentioned above, Baron E. de Demuin who wrote *L'Histoire Religieuse de Jersey*. These works all shed a great deal of light on the plight of the clergy and nobility in Jersey at this time, and give us an insight into living conditions, local response, and attempts by the priests and clergymen to adapt to life on the Island. In recent times, Father Francis P. Isherwood's significant contribution to research here in Jersey,[20] and a book by Joseph Toussaint, *La déportation du clergé de Coutances et Avranches à la Révolution*,[21] have played a noteworthy role in the charting of historical detail.

Signed portrait of Chateaubriand found in Jersey house
(Private Collection)

De La Salle Brothers

The first record we have in Jersey of the presence of Brothers of the Christian Schools (*Frères des Ecoles Chrétiennes*, also known as Lasallians or De La Salle Brothers) dates back to 1792. The Order, founded in 1680 by Jean-Baptiste de la Salle (1651-1719) aimed at improving and organising Christian education for less fortunate children, and was the first religious community of men in the Roman Catholic Church not to include clergy, the Institute comprising solely of lay brothers. As the French Revolution began to outcast more and more religious orders, the Lasallian Brothers found themselves faced with the choice of signing the oath of allegiance to the new civil church or accept prison, exile or death. We know that a small number of Brothers did take the oath and were then severely admonished by their superiors; these included a group of Brothers from Bayeux who actually received their reprimand in writing from St. Helier, the Bishop of Bayeux, Mgr de Cheylus, having been in exile in the Island since December 1st 1791.

It is understood that most Brothers did not sign the oath; many went into hiding, others fled, either to Italy or England, some were imprisoned, as was the case of their Superior General, Frère Agathon. Two Brothers came to Jersey; the first to arrive was Frère Omer (Samson Lafresnée), and his name appears on the list of those receiving help from the *Comité de Secours* in London. The other was Frère Germain (Antoine Joseph Laporte) from Picardy who arrived in Jersey on September 14th 1792 and took lodgings with a certain Sieur Jean Hérault. The Bishop of Bayeux paid him the sum of £9 on October 12th, the help having been accorded by the *Comité de Secours*. He received subsidy until 1799, and in 1803 he was still in Jersey – he had in fact opened a small school for French language studies. It is not known how long he stayed after that date, but one can assume he returned to France shortly after that date along with many others who were allowed to resume work in their dioceses.

Dioceses, Chapels and Oratories

The Second Catholic Relief Act, also known as the Bill of Tolerance, was passed by the British Parliament on June 24th 1791. For the first time since the Reformation, Catholics were allowed to open up chapels and places of worship provided they swore an oath accepting the conditions of the Bill.[22] When the *émigrés* first landed in Jersey, there were no Catholic establishments at all; in fact, as Demuin states in his work, Catholicism had effectively been dead for many years. Apart from a few lacunae during the Reformation – such as under the reign of Queen Mary and again under King James II – it was the austere form of Protestantism advocated by the Geneva-based French exile Jean Calvin[23] which had largely dominated the Island's religious state; this being ever since the influx of the Sixteenth Century Huguenot *réfugiés de religion*. And as if history were once more sweeping circles around the Island, Jersey now found itself welcoming (albeit reluctantly in certain sectors of the community) men and women of a faith whose own ancestors had found themselves banished from our shores two centuries earlier.

Tolerance for Catholics on the British mainland only began to return once the First Catholic Relief Bill of 1778 had been passed. Yet it took at least a year after the Second Relief Bill of 1791 for an active response to the *émigrés'* need for a place of worship in Jersey. The mixed feelings have to be understood: after all, not since the Reformation's huge impact on the Catholic Church in the Sixteenth Century had Jersey witnessed such major and sudden upheavals within the religious order of affairs. Sudden change was hard to accept by some, especially in a small place, and it is interesting to note that many of the supposedly objective history books written in Jersey as late as the mid-19th Century still cast a negative view on the Catholic Church.[24]

There was also a great deal of confusion at the time of the 1791 Relief Bill regarding the diocese Jersey actually belonged to. All through the Middle Ages, the Channel Islands formed part of the French Diocese of Coutances. In 1496 King Henry VII requested Pope Alexander VI to transfer them to Salisbury. Three years later he asked to have them transferred to the Diocese of Winchester. The Pope did as Henry asked – but the Pope's Bull had no effect. Right up to the reign of Elizabeth I the Bishop of Coutances exercised jurisdiction over the Islands. In 1569 the then Bishop of Coutances was on a diplomatic mission in London. He complained that the dues from the Island's Deaneries were not forthcoming. The Privy Council unearthed the Bull and the Royal Letter of 1499; an order in Council of 11th March 1569 executed the separation of the Islands from the Diocese of Coutances and placed them under the jurisdiction of the Anglican

Bishop of Winchester – but once again the Order had no effect. The authority of the Bishop of Winchester was completely ignored owing to the fact that Presbyterian discipline and church government were firmly established in the Islands.

When the Catholic Church in England was placed by Rome under the care of Vicars Apostolic, the Channel Islands were looked after by the Vicar Apostolic of the London District (although it is not clear if they were ever formally included in the territory of his jurisdiction). Bishop John Douglass, who was Vicar Apostolic from 1790 to 1812, appointed Père Charles de Grimouville, an English speaking priest in charge in Jersey in 1807, as Vicar General for Catholic Administration in the Channel Islands; in 1817 he was appointed Bishop of St Malo but died that same year before taking up his post. In 1851, the Channel Islands became part of the newly created Diocese of Southwark. [25]

Part of the uncertainty for historians is due to the fact that amongst the early *émigrés* were five bishops, these being Mgr Augustin Le Mintier de St-André (Bishop of Tréguier), Mgr Joseph Dominic de Cheylus (Bishop of Bayeux), Mgr Alexandre-Henri de Chauvigny de Blot (Bishop of Lombez), Mgr Jean François de la Marche (Bishop of Saint Pol de Léon) and Mgr François Barreau de Girac (Bishop of Rennes). The Bishop of Dol, Mgr Urbain-René de Hercé, also passed through Jersey. The bishops tried to introduce a structure of Church government similar to that existing in their own dioceses; furthermore, the bishops agreed that the liturgy of the Bayeux Diocese should be used in deference to Mgr de Cheylus who was the oldest. [26] In addition, the bishops of Tréguier and Bayeux were both acting as Vicars General for the Bishop of Coutances, and as we read earlier, Jersey was in many respects morally attached to the Diocese of Coutances in spite of all the legal attempts to wrench the Channel Islands away from it!

The priests in Jersey, some alone and others in small groups, soon became missionaries, but it took until September 1792 for the Governor of Jersey to permit the growing numbers of Catholic *émigrés* to actually open places of worship. The arrival of a number of wealthy emigrants gave the refugees the chance to work towards building their own chapel, but this was not to happen for some time yet. In the meantime, four small oratories were finally opened in private houses in St. Helier that year, these being:

1. Chapel of St. Malo – with Chanoine Jean Le Saout, archpriest of St. Malo's Cathedral;
2. Chapel of St. Louis (The Port Chapel) with Père Charles Derbrée, parish priest of Sougéal (Diocese of Rennes);
3. Our Lady and the Holy Angels, with Père Le Roussel de Vaucelles, Superior of the Great Seminary of Evreux;
4. Sacred Heart Chapel, with Père Ange Fournier de la Chateigneraie, Rector of Maure (Diocese of St. Malo).

St. Peter's Chapel in St. Aubin was also opened by Père Vittel, and it is believed there were places of worship in Gorey (opened by priests from Maine and Anjou) and in Trinity where a date-stone was discovered bearing the inscription St-1792-TH, suggesting a place of worship dedicated to St. Thomas.

Whilst these chapels gave the *émigrés* the chance to worship in exile, none of the priests was permitted to actually preach and teach, and in many respects this did not fully respect the 1791 Catholic Relief Bill's new level of tolerance. Jersey's Catholics had not been granted the same freedom of speech and movement as their colleagues on the British mainland. In addition, local Catholic priests were not permitted to convert local Jersey people to the Catholic faith, and this law was re-iterated in a law dated 25th January 1794 published by the Court of London. It specifically forbade Catholic priests from attempting

> to make any impression on the minds of the inhabitants in what concerns religion, also to attack the principles of the Protestant religion now established in the Island.[27]

Matthieu de Gruchy (1761-1797)

One Jerseyman who both protested at the delays in implementing the laws in Jersey and attempted to convert his countrymen was Matthieu de Gruchy (also known in English as Matthew de Gruchy). De Gruchy was a Jerseyman, born on August 31st 1761 at La Maison du Buisson, St. Saviour, to Philippe de Gruchy and his wife Anne du Feu.[28] His parents were both Protestants, and as is explained in l'Abbé du Tressay's 295-page book *Vie de Matthieu de Gruchy*,[29] his two uncles, both merchants in St. Helier, longed for him to become an Anglican minister.

Stained-glass window by Roger Degas in the Parish Church of Saint-Mars-la-Réorthe depicting the execution of Matthieu de Gruchy in 1797 (Courtesy of the Town Hall of Saint-Mars-la-Réorthe)

However, de Gruchy wanted to travel abroad and widen his horizons. In 1776 he set sail for England, a year later sailing on to France in a boat which was captured by French seamen. It was during his captivity that he fell gravely ill, and at this point decided he wanted to convert to Catholicism. He was able to make his first communion whilst in prison, and upon his release was sent to a priest in Angers who hid him from anti-clerical pursuit.

In 1782 he travelled through the village of Saint-Mars-La-Réorthe, building a pulpit for the church there, and his legacy is still active in the whole district.[30] In 1784 he was able to start his studies to become a priest, and on Easter Eve 1788 he was ordained priest. In many respects, as Tina Spencer-Nairn points out in her brief history published by St. Matthew's Church, his ordination was "the germ of resurrection for Catholic life in the Island of Jersey."[31] Based at Soullans, Bois-de-Céné and Beauvoir-sur-Mer[32] where he now was Curate, he too became affected by the impending French Revolution, and when faced with the Constitutional Oath in July 1790, he, like many of the other clergy members around him, refused to sign it. He consequently became obliged to seek refuge, first at Montaigu, then at Boitissandeau Castle.

He too found himself deported to Jersey, having been condemned by the decree of August 26th 1792 which forced those who had not signed the Constitutional Oath to leave the country or face imprisonment. His mission was to travel to England; the Catholic Relief Bill, having been passed in 1791, meant that he could now obtain a certificate to practice his religion and preach to others as a priest. He duly went to the mainland and swore the new oath in accordance with the Bill. However, much to his astonishment he discovered on his return to Jersey on 22nd June 1793, that the laws passed in Britain had not been propagated in the Island.

Keen to open an oratory of his own, his plans were thwarted by Protestant hostilities, and he decided to work as a farmer and convert people he worked amongst. However, a St. Martin farmer named Grandin, whose daughters de Gruchy had converted, ordered the authorities to explain why, as a Jerseyman, he had not been called into the Militia. He was arrested as a deserter. He refused to bear arms, and finally obtained a dispensation. However, as is explained in Balleine's *History of Jersey*:

His conversion of two more girls, Elisabeth and Suzanne Pinel, in 1795, caused the Court to arrest the Bishop of Tréguier for not keeping his clergy in order. This threw the refugees into a panic and de Gruchy was hurried out of the Island.[33]

From Southampton, he travelled back to France and risked his life a number of times whilst ministering in La Vendée. His aim being to return to Jersey and convert his mother to Catholicism, he travelled to Nantes and tried to obtain a passport. It was here that another priest, who himself had signed the Constitutional Oath, recognised him and betrayed him to the French authorities. He was condemned to death. As he was led to his execution, he called for the priest in question and said:

> In handing me over to the Tribunal and having me condemned to death you thought you were causing me some great harm. I look on you rather as the cause of my happiness. He who so wanted to die for us upon the Cross has taught me to forgive, as I do now, asking him to have pity on you and me.[34]

He was executed on Viarmes Square in Nantes on November 28th 1797. Considered a martyr by Catholics, Matthieu de Gruchy's name became immortalised when St. Matthew's Catholic Church at Coin Varin was built some seventy years later.

The Chapels Close

Back in the mid-1790s, the clergy were still living under a considerable amount of tension in Jersey. Admittedly, they had private oratories for their own worship, and a number of ordinations took place in the Island. However, as mentioned earlier, the priests were strictly forbidden to convert Protestants. In addition, attempts were made to make the French priests join the army as soldiers. The Bishops of Bayeux, Dol and Tréguier protested, and as reported by Demuin, sent the Commander in Chief a report stating they would not bear arms.

Some of the priests stayed in Jersey for nearly a decade, others passed through the Island before moving to England. Some dared to return to France and risked the consequences of such a move. Mgr de Hercé,

Bishop of Dol, was one such man, and he was shot in Vannes in 1795.

Others died in Jersey, and this caused some confusion regarding suitable burial places. As there was no Catholic cemetery in the Island, many were buried at Les Mielles Cemetery (which no longer exists and was replaced by All Saints Church). Others found resting places elsewhere. Bishop Cheylus of Bayeux died in Jersey in 1797 aged 80, and was interred at St. Saviour's Cemetery where other *émigrés* were also buried.[35] It was not until much later, in 1854, that Almorah Cemetery was built for non-conformists in Jersey, and it now houses many graves belonging to Catholic orders that stayed in the Island.

The political climate was changing in France, and after Napoleon Bonaparte's *coup d'état* in 1799 commonly referred to as the coup of 18 Brumaire, the oppression of the French clergy began to subside in France; by the beginning of the nineteenth Century, many of the priests decided to return to their homes, knowing that they could preach and worship without the fear of persecution. In 1801, the Concordat was signed. The Concordat was an agreement between Napoleon Bonaparte and Pope Pius VII which re-established the Roman Catholic Church in France. Napoleon took the initiative in negotiating this agreement; he recognized that reconciliation with the church was of political benefit to him – it would help consolidate his position, end the royalist-clerical rebellion in western France, reunite the clergy, which had been divided since the French Revolution, and win the support of the large majority of peasant-farmers. By its terms Roman Catholicism was recognized as the religion of most French citizens, but not the official religion. Archbishops and bishops were to be nominated by the government, but the Pope was to confer the office. Parish priests were to be appointed by the bishops, subject to government approval. Confiscated church property, most of which had been sold to private persons, was not to be restored, but the government was to provide adequate support for the clergy. To implement the Concordat Napoleon issued the so-called Organic Articles in 1802; these restated the traditional liberties of the Gallican church while increasing Napoleon's control of church activities. The Organic Articles were not agreed to by the Pope, and he did not consider them binding. The Concordat was in force until 1905.

As a consequence of the exodus back to France, the oratories began to close down. The priests, Père Le Saout and Père de la Chateigneraye returned to their dioceses in 1801, and the small chapels of the Sacré

Coeur and St. Malo were shut. St. Louis' Chapel closed on May 4th 1801 when Père Guérin of St-Sylvain (Bayeux) returned to France, and the final chapel to close was Our Lady and the Holy Angels in July 1803.

A New Chapel

Many priests had left, but a few men of the cloth still remained. In addition, a large number of the non-clerical refugees decided to stay in the Island. This left a growing need for a new Catholic chapel, and in September 1803, the discontinued oratories were replaced by an old flour loft in Castle Street which they rented. The premises were by no means luxurious, and access to the chapel was via a ladder. The chapel was dedicated to St. Louis in memory of the king, and was commonly known as *Les Mielles* (The Sand Hills). Père Jean-François Philibert, Parish Priest of Mesnil-Ranfray (Avranches) was in charge of the mission.

However, until this time, the only form of Mass which had been permitted was Low Mass. But shortly after March 21st 1804, when the Duke of Enghien, the last descendant of the Bourbons, was executed at the Château de Vincennes on Napoleon's orders, an act regarded by most monarchists as murder, the Jersey *émigré* community wanted to hold a Requiem Mass for the Duke. In many ways, this event was a huge catalyst for the local Catholics. Concerned by anti-Catholic behaviour in Jersey, Père Philibert invited the Governor of Jersey and the authorities of the Island to attend the service; and because they did attend, this in itself reduced much of the antagonism the *émigrés* felt with regard to their faith. This event also enabled them to start holding whatever type of Mass they desired.

When Père Philibert returned to France in 1807, he was replaced by the English-speaking Père de Grimouville who then asked Père F. Le Guédois, the assistant priest of Saussey in Coutances, to take charge of the Mission.[36] He was succeeded by Père Jean-Charles Pagny who died in Jersey in November 1822 and was buried, like so many other Catholics, at Les Mielles Cemetery.

By this time, a growing population of Irish workers had settled in Jersey, and they shared the same chapel at St. Louis with the French. According to Demuin's reports, there was continual friction between

The altar at the original St. Thomas' Church (formerly Albion Chapel)
in New Street
Glass plate photograph from 1879 (Courtesy of St. Thomas' Church)

the two groups, and things were only resolved when pleas to Bishop William Poynter in London finally resulted in the building of a chapel for the Irish. This was in 1826, and their Hue Street Chapel was the first Catholic place of worship to be built in Jersey since the Reformation.

The French also realised that their own congregation was getting too big for the old flour loft at Les Mielles. The Castle Street chapel needed a successor, and it was through Père J. Morlais, the assistant priest of Dol who came to Jersey in September 1837, that Albion Chapel, the former Anabaptist chapel in New Street, was purchased by the French Catholic community through the agency of a Jersey resident – it was still forbidden for foreigners to buy land in Jersey at that time. The Bishop of the London District at that time was Mgr Thomas Griffiths, and as the refurbishment and reconstruction of the old building progressed, his help and guidance were fully acknowledged by the community who decided to place the new chapel under the patronage of the Apostle Saint Thomas. It was opened for worship on October 23rd 1842.

Major changes were happening within Catholic life in the Island. In 1845 more improvements took place in the chapel, and to the relief of all Catholics, the Pope re-established the Ecclesiastical Hierarchy in England in 1850; things were looking bright. But this did not necessarily please many Protestants in Jersey, and according to the historian Jean de la Croix, a plan was hatched by those opposed to the rise of Catholicism to actually burn down the two Catholic churches – St. Mary's which had been built at Vauxhall for the Irish community, and St. Thomas' in New Street. The conspiracy was foiled, and the Governor of Jersey even had troops from Fort Regent brought in to quell the plot.

A new chapter in Catholic life in Jersey was about to start. St. Thomas' Chapel in New Street certainly marked the beginning of a new era for the French, who by now were integrating into Jersey life. Those who had stayed in the Island were no longer *émigrés* anxious to return home, but were making Jersey their new abode; consequently it was necessary to widen the horizons and look at how further expansion and missionary education could enhance their quality of life.

2   Expansion and Education

A New Parish – St. Martin's

The establishment of St. Thomas' Parish in St. Helier had been a success for the Catholic community. However, as many of the French and Irish Catholics living in Jersey were lodged in rural areas of the Island – a vast number of the French were on farms or placed in houses as domestics, and many of the Irish were based near St. Catherine's where they were working on the Breakwater – there arose a fresh need for expansion. In 1847, a French priest from Bordeaux, Père E. Hallum, came to Jersey principally for health reasons, and stayed at Carteret View House at Faldouet, St. Martin. When he realized that for most people living in the countryside, a trip into St. Helier to attend Mass would mean a 5-7 mile journey, he decided to set up a small chapel and school on a plot of land adjacent to the house at Faldouet, and laid the foundation stone that very same year, the aim being to give the approximately 550 Catholics in St. Martin (and their children) the opportunity to access their faith through prayer and education. The chapel was named Notre Dame de Saint Martin and, albeit in an unofficial capacity Père Hallum worked there for eight years.

In 1851, the French Catholics on the east of the Island sent a petition to the Bishop of Southwark, asking for an official mission to be set up in the Parish of St. Martin. They underlined the fact that the Catholic Church on the Island was still too centralized for most of those who lived in the countryside, and that efforts needed to be made to prevent Catholics from either abandoning their faith or from converting to Protestantism purely for topographical reasons.

What shall be said of the domestic servants who make up most of the Catholic population in the country? Their plight is even

The Church of Our Lady of the Annunciation and Martyrs of Japan,
St. Martin

more painful. Their non-Catholic masters, full of misguided good will, would say to them: "There is a chapel not far from here, go there if you wish, but we cannot really allow you to have any more time off".[1]

Père Hallum also wrote a letter to Bishop Thomas Grant of Southwark, expressing his concern over the way the priests in St. Helier (from the two parishes already existing) were behaving with regards to the St. Martin project. Nobody seemed willing to help out in the rural parts of the Island, fearful of losing their congregation in town. This, added Père Hallum, had given rise to a number of taunts being made by local Protestants with regard to petty squabbling within the Catholic Church.

On April 15th 1855, Père Hallum wrote to Bishop Grant to tell him he was leaving Jersey; still no priest arrived to take charge of the Chapel in St. Martin, so another petition was prepared in 1856. This time, the petition was signed by a certain "Benoit" who took the initiative of sending it directly to the French Emperor, Napoleon III. It proved effective: the petition was first sent to the Archbishop of Paris, then the Bishop of Southwark, who consequently appointed Père Joseph Guiramand from the Avignon Diocese; he became priest in charge of the Catholic Mission of Our Lady in St. Martin.

Within a few months, Père Guiramand was able to start work on refurbishing Père Hallum's old chapel, and on September 6th 1857, the chapel was officially blessed.

It proved such a success that expansion was once again on the cards; the only stumbling block was funding. The parishioners were mostly poor working-class people, and money was scarce. Père Guiramand wrote to all the French Bishops and a number of nobles in France and Europe, and response soon poured in. Even the Queen of Portugal offered the sum of £20. Most of the large churches in Paris contributed; Napoleon III sent a monstrance with the imperial arms engraved on its foot, and his wife, the Empress Eugenie, a set of Stations of the Cross. On September 3rd 1862, he was able to inform the Bishop of Southwark that the foundation stone had been laid, and that the roof of the new church would be erected by Christmas. Completed in February 1863, the church was blessed by Bishop Grant in June 1863 and given the name of Our Lady of the Annunciation and Martyrs of

Japan, the name it still bears to this day.

The reference to the Martyrs of Japan may appear puzzling, yet the explanation is quite logical. The first Christian missionaries sent to Japan arrived in the country in 1547, preaching the Gospel and baptizing many converts. However, when Christianity was banned in Japan later that century, persecutions began to take place, the most well-known being that of six Franciscans, three Jesuits and seventeen laymen who were crucified in Nagasaki on February 5th 1597. The twenty-six martyrs were beatified in 1627 and canonized by Pope Pius IX in June 1862, their feast arranged for February 3rd. The first feast coincided with the completion of the new church in St. Martin's, which therefore would explain Père Guiramand's choice.

Stone Tablet to mark the Consecration of
Our Lady Church, St. Martin: June 1863

A Hybrid Island

By the mid-Nineteenth Century, the influx of foreigners and refugees from all walks of life had led to a hybrid population in the Island. Although Jersey remained dominated by Protestantism, many new denominations had established themselves along with their own places of worship – Methodism was on the rise, and over thirty chapels were built island-wide; their faith, like others, was met with violence on more than one occasion. Other churches and temples including meeting places for the Independent Church, Bible Christians, Presbyterians, Baptists, Quakers, Plymouth Brethren, Unitarians, Swedenborgians, Mormons, plus a Jewish synagogue were set up, and in spite of frequent clashes, everyone seemed to be able to have some form of freedom of worship in the Island. Even Jersey's most famous French visitor in exile, the great writer Victor Hugo (who stayed here for just over three years between 1852 and 1855) was able, on more than one stormy occasion, to vent his feelings about established religion, most specifically against the Catholic Church,[2] and although he also criticised the latent Puritanism in Jersey, he nevertheless realised that people's beliefs could be expressed without fear of persecution:

> Sunday is the only flaw in the island's love of liberty [...] Churches and chapels are everywhere. Every sect is represented – in Jersey there is even a Mormon chapel.[3]

With the growth of the population, Jersey was having to learn that freedom of speech came at a price, and in order to co-habit, religious tolerance would have to be nurtured amongst its people.

1863 – Further Expansion

In 1860, Père Morlais (who had instigated the purchase of the Anabaptist chapel which became St. Thomas' in St. Helier), was forced to retire due to ill-health, and he was replaced by a dynamic missionary Belgian priest named Père Jean François Volkeryck;[4] both Demuin the historian and more recent writers agree that he can be regarded as the founder of modern Catholicism in Jersey.

To his consternation, he realised that despite the fact that many Catholics were attending Mass, nothing was being done for their education. At this time there were about 5000 Catholics in St. Thomas' Parish alone. Faced with "no presbytery, no parish school and no funding to create them either",[5] he realised that outside help was needed. Little did he know at this stage just how influential his choice of aid would become. In Bruges, Belgium, a school had recently been opened by the *Dames de Saint-André*, a missionary order.[6] He contacted the Superior General, and on June 20th 1863, an agreement was signed. The *Dames de Saint-André* were to come to Jersey as missionaries and help set up a school in the Parish of St. Thomas.

Les Dames de Saint-André

Established by two Belgian Sisters in 1231, the congregation of *Les Dames de Saint-André* started out as a charitable hospice in the town of Tournai, caring for the sick, the poor as well as pilgrims returning from the Holy Land. On October 28th 1249, their existence was officially acknowledged in a Bull signed by Pope Innocent IV. By 1329, the Order built a chapel dedicated to St. Andrew on their site, and their nursing work expanded. Until the 17th Century, the Order was largely founded on Augustine principles, and it was not until after major changes in the infrastructure of the monastery, largely brought about by the effects of the Reformation, that the constitution of the Order began to change. Firstly, from being a hospice, the monastery transformed itself into a cloistered community, focusing principally on spiritual growth. Secondly, the arrival in 1643 of a Jesuit priest, Père Antoine Civoré, sent to revise the constitution, led to a gradual change in spiritual tendency, and as time went by, the Order became closely linked with the teachings of Saint Ignatius of Loyola.

It was only on the eve of the French Revolution that they moved away from their cloistered existence and entered the domain of missionary education, firstly by taking in pupils and setting up a school at their monastery, and then finding themselves forced into the wide world. Being based in Belgium the Order was not affected by the Revolution at first, but by 1796 the Sisters were forcibly expelled from the monastery and obliged to go into hiding. It was not until Napoleon took over in 1801 that the Order was allowed to return; the Sisters were able to buy back part of their building and continue their work. From that point onwards, the Order became more and more closely associated with the Society of Jesus and in 1857 they adopted the Jesuit constitution and headed towards missionary work both within Belgium and abroad.

As the highly informative book *Les Religieuses de Saint-André* tells us, the first three nuns left for Jersey on July 21st 1863, arriving in the Island three days later.[7] They were under the leadership of Mère Emilie Daumelye, and settled into premises in Duhamel Street. By October, the school was ready to take in the first pupils, and from an initial group of 56 children, the school rapidly gained 100 regular pupils. Once again, the question of expansion loomed, and until a larger building could be found to accommodate them, they rented an attic; conditions were cramped for all. As we are informed both in Demuin's work and in the 1908 study on the *Dames de Saint-André*:

> The parlour could barely contain a few chairs; after meals the tiny refectory served as a community and study room. The Superior's room served both as classroom and sacristy during the day, and the nuns had their lodgings in the attic. As for the chapel, it could barely fit eight people.[8]

To start with, the nuns were given a very positive welcome by most Jersiais, and some episodes proved to be quite amusing:

> At first, their trips to church gave rise to some comic scenes which, however, soon turned tragic. On the whole, the Jersiais just expressed a sense of benevolent curiosity towards them, assuming that Mother Emilie was a respectable mother who had come to Jersey with her daughters (the other nuns!) to open a school. Their unusual clothing attracted attention, so much so that these flocks of inquisitive people would line up on the roadsides to watch them go past. Listening to their comments the nuns could sometimes hardly contain their laughter.[9]

However, as the above quote implies, their smiles soon turned to tears. When it became known that these ladies were Catholic nuns who had come to Jersey to compete with Protestant schools, some reactions were violent. Stones were hurled through their windows, and they even needed police protection when going to church. Another example of the need for tolerance within the Island community.

In spite of the resentment they occasionally encountered, they managed to make headway, and by January 1864 they had opened a third section at the school. An interesting fact regarding the education structure is that class divisions were upheld quite firmly within the establishment, this being to allow as many poor children as possible to receive free Catholic education whilst the more affluent families paid for their children's education. Non-paying – or poor - pupils were segregated from those whose parents paid fees; and those parents who could afford more than 6d a week would be allowed to see their children receive their education in yet a different class within the school. This also allowed the Sisters to plan the education in such a way that lessons would have a better degree of consistency for those who attended full-time. One must not forget the fact that many of the parents of poorer children needed to remove their children from class when the planting and harvesting of potatoes took place; this inevitably interrupted their schooling, but it was a basic fact of rural existence at that time. In addition, many Breton farm workers would come to Jersey for brief periods, essentially to earn more money during the busier farming periods; this too increased the floating population within the Island and its education system.

The work undertaken by the *Dames de Saint-André* was regarded with such high regard by both the Bishop of Southwark and their own Superior General in Belgium that not only was another nun sent to help at Duhamel Street, but they were given the permission to move into another larger house. In 1866, they moved out and rented more spacious premises at Albion House in New Street, letting the Lasallian *Frères de l'Ecole Chrétienne* (who had recently arrived in the Island) take over the Duhamel Street premises.

Education for Boys

Since 1855 the Lasallian (De La Salle) Brothers had been living in London, at 49 Clapham High Street. This was the first De La Salle Foundation in England, opened just five years after the restoration of the Catholic hierarchy in Britain: a group of French Brothers had set up a school called Saint Joseph's College in Clapham for a mixed clientele of English and French boys.

Père Volkeryck had first approached them in 1861, shortly before he had made contact with the *Dames de Saint-André*. He had hoped they would come over to Jersey to open a school. To start with, the Brothers refused; over the next few years Père Volkeryck continued to send requests, hoping to open a school for the sons of Breton seasonal workers, and it was only when Père Volkeryck secured the help of Mgr David, Bishop of St. Brieuc and later Mgr Grant of Southwark, that he saw any result. As Brother Edward[10] explains in his Diary:

> In 1866 he informed the Brother Superior that he was still awaiting the Brothers and added that he had ready for them, a furnished house, linen, and a yearly income of £28! Faced with such determination, Brother Philippe finally gave way, and sent four Brothers from London in October 1866. Rev. Brother Thomas of Canterbury was at their head. This man must have had outstanding qualities, for he was only twenty-three and a half years of age. Within a matter of weeks, he was popular among the people, important and unimportant. The idea of a school for the Breton Catholics disappeared. Children of all faiths flocked to the school, and within two months it contained over one hundred pupils.[11]

Within two years Brother Thomas had to retire from exhaustion. He was replaced by Brother Abban, and subsequently Brother Alban, whose teaching skills not only inspired the pupils, but bewitched the neighbours who would lean out of their windows or even sit on the window sills in order to listen to his lessons.

Movement at Albion House

In the meantime, the *Dames de Saint-André* settled into Albion House, and Mère Journet, the Superior General in Belgium, corresponded with Père Volkeryck with regards to expanding even further, the next plan being to buy and even construct a permanent school, convent and chapel in St. Helier. However, in February 1870, she died and was replaced by Mère Lucie. Her chief task was to continue the work of her predecessor and establish not only a larger school for girls in St. Helier, but tend to the needs of the rural parishes. She visited Jersey and inspected the new premises, a large house called Monséjour, centrally located at David Place / Val Plaisant, which would need considerable redesigning and construction work, but which would become their permanent base.

The façade runs along the busiest street in St. Helier; the building is accessed by three flights of stairs with Gothic balustrades topped with a delightful hexagonal turret. The view from the eaves stretches over the town as far as the sea; the rooftop is also fashioned in an elaborate Gothic style, and gives this solid building of unique pink Jersey granite a most elegant crown.[12]

Le Couvent St-André / Convent FCJ at David Place
(Copyright © Jersey Evening Post)

The architect behind the building's new appearance was Alfred-Louis Frangeul, a renowned architect from St. Malo.[13] This was not to be his only work in Jersey for the Catholic community. The major works were over by April 4th 1874 and the Sisters were able to take possession of the premises along with 212 pupils.[14] On November 5th that year, Bishop James Danell of Southwark blessed the chapel in the presence of local priests and the French Consul. The De La Salle Brothers then moved into Albion House in New Street. The school for girls became known as *Le Couvent Saint-André* (St. André's Convent), and the boys' school, was called St. Thomas' Elementary School. Both schools flourished under the Sisters and Brothers.

In the years leading up to the construction of the new building at Val Plaisant, the *Dames de Saint-André* had also taken over the running of the girls' education at the Irish Vauxhall School, sending three nuns there each day as from October 1869. Furthermore, their work was not limited to school teaching; as Père Vincent Igoa (the last French Oblate to serve in Jersey) points out in his book *A Hundred Years of Life in Jersey*:

> They gave instruction to the converts, helped in organising religious services in the parish, such as First Communion, processions, the distribution of clothes to poor children, money collected by the Sisters and their helpers through bazaars and collections for parishioners in need.[15]

By 1875, Père Volkeryck had also enabled the *Congrégation des Enfants de Marie* (Children of Mary) to be established in St. Helier; the education of boys by the De La Salle Brothers continued to prosper within the Parish; a Saint Vincent-de-Paul Conference for ladies to help the poor was also started by Père Volkeryck with the assistance of the *Dames de Saint-André*, who had their Society of Ladies of Charity; a Parish Library was also opened at the Convent. Teamwork had proven to be effective, and, as we shall discover later in this work, the involvement of the *Dames de Saint-André* in Jersey life would go from strength to strength.

Financial Aid

In 1877 Brother Alban left St. Thomas' School to work in Montreal. The year of his departure marked another interesting event. For the first time, a school established by the Brothers in the Channel Islands received financial aid from a Government. It took the shape of a grant of 500 francs from the French Government, this being in view of the fact that a great number of the pupils at the school were sons of

Frenchmen who had moved to Jersey. The success of this school was another accomplishment for Père Volkeryck, and at this particular stage, nothing seemed to be able to impede further developments.

The Church Moves West – St. Matthew's Parish

In many respects, Père Volkeryck's mission had only just begun. Fuelled by the success in St. Thomas' Parish, he decided to explore the west of the Island. Aware that there was no Catholic Church west of St. Helier, and conscious of the fact that many French families lived on that side of the Island, he decided to build a church, boys' school and presbytery on a plot of land which could also have farming potential, thus guaranteeing some revenue for the Church. He raised money and in 1869 tried to get permission to buy a site at Carrefour Selous, at the meeting point of three parishes: St. Peter, St. Lawrence and St. Mary. It is believed that the Constable of St. Lawrence, aware that the site was officially in his parish, expressed concern that a Papist establishment might be erected on his soil, so ultimately the land Père Volkeryck was allowed to purchase was a little further away, situated in St. Peter at Coin Varin. This did not seem to perturb the authorities of this parish. When Père Volkeryck visited the plot of land, he is understood to have been ecstatic: "It is here I wish to erect a temple to the Lord!" he is said to have exclaimed.[16] The land was purchased through the help of benefactors, and the foundation stone of the church was laid on May 23rd 1871. The ceremony was presided over by a former minister of Napoleon III, Edouard Drouyn de l'Huys, who had sought refuge in Jersey after the events of September 4th 1870 which had led to France once more becoming a Republic.[17] His speech praised the hospitality of Jersey and the unifying power of faith:

> I cannot help but feel emotional seeing myself here amongst you, on foreign soil, inaugurating the foundation of this church [...]
>
> How can it be, that I, hurled by the storm onto these shores, a mere fortuitous visitor to your hospitable island, have found myself invited to one of the most cherished moments of your existence? We might be reminded us of what Ruth said to Naomi; "Your people are my people, and your God is my God". [...]

*St. Matthew's Church
at the beginning of the
1900s
(Courtesy of Mike
Edmunds)*

Religious feeling is one of the most powerful bonds between men. Gathered together from every point of the compass, we meet in the land where souls are no longer bound by physical or political frontiers, and we are like those navigators who have set off from totally opposite ends of the globe and reach the same port, purely because they have followed the same star in the sky.[18]

Père Volkeryck then explained why the name Matthew had been chosen. It was only natural, he felt, that this new place of worship should pay homage to the memory of the Jersey martyr Matthieu de Gruchy who was executed in 1797. This new church was to be designed in neo-Gothic style, with one nave and tribune, transepts and an apse, and he hoped the construction work would be completed within eighteen months.

The choice of architect was not insignificant. Alfred-Louis Frangeul of St. Malo who had redesigned the new convent at David Place for the *Dames de Saint-André*, was one of the most prolific and acclaimed architects in Brittany, having already built a number of churches in the region; he worked mainly with neo-Gothic Thirteenth-Century designs, the exact style Père Volkeryck had desired. At this stage, the funding would not cover costly stained-glass windows; these were added at a later date.[19] The builders Blampied and Holloway met their deadline, and the church was ready to be opened and blessed on September 4th 1872, a ceremony which took place in the presence of Bishop James Danell of Southwark and Bishop Félix Fournier of Nantes. Not since before the Reformation had Mass been held in the north-west of Jersey. Shortly afterwards, the granite building housing the school and presbytery was completed.

The early years were hard, and although one of the Parish priests from St. Thomas' travelled to St. Matthew's every Saturday evening in order to spend the night there, celebrate Mass on the Sunday morning, give the children their catechism lesson, the new Parish of St. Matthew's struggled to keep going. Within eight years, the buildings began to deteriorate, and with no more than forty pupils at the school, no permanent priest, and no funding, the future of St. Matthew's looked grim.

It appeared that history was repeating itself. Less than twenty years earlier, the fate of St. Martin's Church had almost been identical: the need for a church arose, the collecting of funds succeeded, and the creation of the place of worship was fulfilled. Yet, the priests alone seemed incapable of assuming the combination of leadership and team spirit which was so essential to make the parish thrive. The teamwork so deftly engineered between Père Volkeryck and the *Dames de Saint-André* and De La Salle Brothers in town could not be emulated elsewhere; it became obvious that the rural parishes would need new impetus in order to survive.

More Intolerance in France

As we have seen repeatedly during the course of this section, the past century in French history clearly coloured the influx of arrivals and departures of French *émigrés* to and from Jersey. Whenever a French regime expressed hostility to the Church, more French refugees would arrive here. Each time stability was restored in France, the clergy would leave our shores. These waves of arrivals and departures would be punctuated by the influx of other radically different political refugees (such as Victor Hugo); time after time, Jersey proved to be a crossroads for these men and women escaping some form of persecution.

So let us summarise the past seventy years since Napoleon's demise: the Restoration years in France (1814-1830) had seen a re-establishment of the Catholic Church in France, and by the time the Second Republic commenced (in 1848), the role of the Church was much stronger – most Catholic Orders and congregations flourished during this period. However, this was not to last. Whereas the beginnings of the Second Empire (1851-1870) looked promising, the final years proved to be hard for the Church. In 1851 Louis Napoleon, President of the Second Republic, imitating the tactics of his uncle, Napoleon Bonaparte, made himself Emperor. Anxious to have the support of the Church he gave seats in the Senate to the French Cardinals, and might have succeeded in getting Pope Pius IX to come to Paris to crown him had not the Sovereign Pontiff insisted on the abolition of the Organic Articles. As we saw in Jersey, Napoleon III's support of the Church extended to sending ornate personal gifts to be displayed in St. Martin's Church. However, as the Empire years went by, a spirit of agnosticism spread through society. A Masonic movement aimed at dechristianising the schools (supported by Victor Duruy, the Minister of Public Instruction) was introduced from Belgium in 1866. From 1858 on, the passing of a series of laws curtailing the freedom of action of the Church underlined the Emperor's desire to placate his enemies in order to maintain his power.

In 1870, after the defeat of Napoleon III in the war against Prussia, France once more became a Republic, and anti-clericalism was yet again a leitmotif of the new government's politics. Believing France's education system to be inferior to that in Prussia (hence their defeat in the war), the French government decided to expel religious figures from public schools (expelling 5000 alone on November 29, 1880). By 1881-2 a series of laws known as the Jules Ferry Laws came into being, establishing free but mandatory secular (non-clerical) education. Proposed by the Republican Minister of Public Instruction Jules Ferry, they played an instrumental role in the Third Republic (1871-1940).

Met with mixed feelings throughout the country, these laws clearly threatened the various Catholic Orders and their schools. Many became *émigrés* once again and fled the country, hoping to continue their missions wherever this could be possible. Naturally, the Channel Islands were the ideal geographical and linguistic location for many of these French orders, and soon Jersey was to become home to a number of groups who would effectively revitalise Catholicism in the Island. Leadership and teamwork would combine to advance the cause.

II

Teamwork and Leadership

1880-1900

3   Holy Hill (i)

Helpers of the Holy Souls

By 1880 the political situation in France was tense, and many religious orders decided it safer to leave the country. Jesuit orders in particular were treated unsympathetically as a result of the Jules Ferry Laws recently passed, but in many respects this was nothing particularly new for them. History was forever repeating itself, and most of the new-styled "refugees" who came to Jersey from 1880 knew that what their forefathers had endured had been infinitely worse.

Amongst the first groups to arrive in Jersey in the late spring of 1880 was a small party of three Sisters from Paris. These belonged to an order called *La Société des Auxiliatrices des Ames du Purgatoire*, known in English as Helpers of the Holy Souls. A religious order for women, it was founded in Paris in 1856 by Eugénie Smet (1825-1871) who became better known by her religious name Marie de la Providence. Inspired by the teachings of St. Ignatius de Loyola, the Order decided to adhere to Jesuit rules in 1859, and from that point onwards it was essentially a Jesuit group. Their principal aim being to care for the sick and dying, tend to the poor and pray for souls in purgatory, they also became known for their active involvement in religious instruction and free circulating libraries.

When the three *Auxiliatrices* arrived in Jersey, having been sent from Paris by their Mother General Madeleine de Frazzi, their mission was to find a suitable property for a small group of them to move into and work from, and where ultimately they could set up a novitiate. They spent the first month in a hotel whilst negotiating the purchase of a large house on the outskirts of St. Helier at Wellington Hill known as Beaulieu.[1] This large house had been the property of the Bertram family since it was built in 1825.[2] On June 12th 1880, the property was bought

*Beaulieu: Main House and Chapel. Photograph produced by
the Auxiliatrices des Ames du Purgatoire in 1930
to celebrate fifty years in Jersey
(Courtesy of Gerard Lecrivain)*

by Marie Joseph Burke and Sarah Elizabeth Guy, Jersey residents acting on behalf of the *Auxiliatrices*.

Once established in Jersey under the direction of their Mother Superior Bienheureuse Françoise d'Amboise, the *Auxiliatrices* soon began to work actively in the town area, visiting the sick, both in private homes and at the hospital, teaching in the Catholic schools (St. Thomas' and Vauxhall), and engaging themselves freely in a variety of parish activities. Both adults and children were converted as a result of their teachings, and the Auxiliatrices soon widened their horizons in the Island. This was the kind of impetus that the Catholic community felt was needed, and it complemented the work achieved and pursued by the *Dames de Saint-André* who were still actively increasing their workload within the Parish.

In 1885, now under the supervision of Mère Denis, the Novitiate of the Missions opened, and until 1919 when it was transferred to San Remo (Italy), it operated from Beaulieu.[3] On August 30th 1892, the foundation stone for a new chapel was laid at Beaulieu adjoining the main house. The chapel, built in traditional style, was of pink Jersey granite from the Mont Mado area, and judging from the sheer amount of detail and quality art which went into the creation of the building, was funded by support from the *Auxiliatrices*' motherhouse in Paris; of specific note are the stained glass windows which were installed in 1893. These windows were designed by the renowned Parisian art historian and stained glass expert Edouard Amédée Didron (1836-1902),[4] famed for his numerous works of art in churches and cathedrals, including fifty-eight windows at Notre-Dame de Dijon which he was still completing at the time of the Beaulieu windows. Commissioned and funded by the *Auxiliatrices* in Paris, the windows at Beaulieu Chapel include dramatic portrayals of purgatory as well as symbols reflecting the society's adherence to Jesuit principles.[5]

In 1906, twenty-six years after their arrival in Jersey, Mère Gabriel commissioned a statue of Christ to commemorate the fiftieth anniversary of the founding of the Order. This statue was placed in the grounds of Beaulieu near the main house (and is still there to this day). Created by another famed artist, this time from Lannion in Brittany, Yves Hernot II (1861-1929), carved the statue from local Breton granite and shipped it to Jersey for the *Auxiliatrices*. Of further interest to us is the fact that Hernot's father, Yves Hernot I (1829-

1890) was commissioned to sculpt a memorial piece at Tréguier Cathedral for the tomb of the last Bishop of Tréguier, none other than Mgr Augustin Le Mintier who, as we will recall from the previous section, was one of the *émigré* bishops who fled to Jersey at the time of the French Revolution.[6] The *Auxiliatrices*' choice of sculptor might have been purely coincidental; the Hernots were well-established sculptors of wayside crosses and religious statues, but on the other hand there is a strong possibility that Hernot II was commissioned by the Sisters as a tribute to the previous generations' plight, thus heightening the historical link with Jersey's French Catholic past. The *Auxiliatrices* would have been more than familiar with the reasons for Mgr Le Mintier's presence and actions in the Island, and the symbolism of asking the Hernot I's son to create their Jersey sculpture would have appealed to them.[7]

Statue of Christ at Beaulieu by Yves Hernot II,
commissioned by the Auxiliatrices des Ames du Purgatoire

It is clear that the *Auxiliatrices*, who worked as unpaid volunteers within the community, had considerable monetary support from Paris. Not only were the Sisters able to do their charitable work within the community, but they had enough financial assistance to purchase property, costly windows, decorations and statues. Funds were not a problem for them at this stage, and this was precisely the kind of solid aid the three Jersey parishes needed. As far as the *Auxiliatrices* were concerned, they were as self-sufficient as the *Dames de Saint-André*, and their nursing and educational skills could only enhance the work already being achieved in the Island.

Over the years, the Sisters' role in Catholic education and the healing of the sick (specifically using herbal remedies of their own) expanded, and during the later years, they were equally involved at a number of Protestant schools in St. Helier (St. Luke's, St. Saviour's and Halkett Place) as well as at the Catholic schools (including FCJ as from 1911).[8]

Maison Saint-Louis – the early years

At around the same time as the *Auxiliatrices'* arrival in Jersey, a Jesuit priest named Père Chambellan was sent to Jersey from Paris to try and purchase a large property. It was not the first time that the Society of Jesus had hoped to set up a new base in Jersey. As early as 1828, when a measure taken by the French government against religious orders closed all Jesuit colleges, the Paris Province of the Society sent two priests to the Island to explore various possibilities, fully aware of the potential present in Jersey. Their bid was unsuccessful and the plans were dropped. A new attempt in 1838 met the same fate. Once again, in 1842, with an unsettled anti-clerical atmosphere hovering over France, attempts were made by the Jesuits to settle on the Island, but these were met with a categorical refusal by the States of Jersey. Within eight years, the heated political climate in France had subsided, and by 1850 new legislation introduced by Alfred de Falloux, the Minister of Education, allowed the Roman Catholic Church to resume education without fear of reprisals.

Fast forward thirty years and the new Ferry Laws were severely affecting religious orders throughout France: many seminaries and schools were shut down. The Jesuits knew they had to leave the country. So in the early months of 1880, they decided to try and transfer a major seminary from Laval in Brittany to Jersey, and Père Chambellan's mission was to locate an appropriate establishment where the scholastics could continue their studies. Quite coincidentally, he became aware that the Imperial Hotel, surrounded by expansive grounds on St. Saviour's Road, was for sale, the land itself being the original plot the Jesuits had tried to purchase over fifty years earlier, before the hotel itself had been built.[9] Nevertheless, before attempting to purchase the property, Père Chambellan approached the Bishop of Southwark, Mgr Danell. The bishop was uncertain about the project, fearing that opening a large seminary for Jesuits in Jersey could arouse anti-papist prejudices in the Island – and thus jeopardise the progress the Catholic Church was already making. He suggested they move to another part of his diocese on the mainland. However, the priest in charge of the Irish mission in Jersey, Father Jeremiah McCarthy, opposed this view and gave the Jesuits his total support. A strong-worded letter to Mgr Danell successfully changed the bishop's mind, and ultimately the Imperial Hotel was purchased on June 8th 1880, with Father McCarthy acting as proxy – the French Jesuits, as foreigners, could not purchase property in Jersey, so it was rented to them by fellow Jesuits on the British mainland.

On June 20th 1880, the Jesuits were expelled from their seminary in Laval, and by September 1st, the young men and their teachers started moving to Jersey. Their arrival in small groups did not go unnoticed, and within days of their arrival, a sense of fear began to mount within the Protestant community. Eager to adapt to their new country of residence, the French Jesuits decided to wear British-style "Roman collars" rather than their traditional cassocks. Nevertheless, they were still much more conspicuous than the smaller groups of *Auxiliatrices* who had already settled at Beaulieu, and the Jesuits soon became the centre of attention amongst certain groups of locals. At first, the fears voiced by Mgr Danell when he initially opposed their coming to Jersey, seemed quite prophetic. As Père Charles Rey explained in his 1966 talk *The Jesuits who lived at the Hotel de France*:

> It was rumoured that the Jesuits would bring the Island to ruin by setting up an immense commercial empire. Some women were so frightened by what they heard that they threatened to leave the Island with their families.[10]

Imperial Hotel (Maison Saint-Louis) photographed by Ernest Baudoux
(Courtesy of Peter Abrams)

Furthermore, on August 5th 1880, the Protestant rector of St. Martin lodged a "Projet de Loi au Greffe" to visit all schools set up by the Jesuits. As well as the unfounded claims that the Jesuits had come to bring economic ruin to Jersey, most of the unrest regarding the Jesuits' arrival in Jersey was focused on the fear of them opening new schools all over the Island, a fear which understandably seemed to threaten the very existence of the Protestant schools. For many people, their presence was an invasion, and we must not forget that at almost the same time as they were setting up their seminary in Jersey, preparations were being made for the centenary of the Battle of Jersey. Locals were being constantly reminded of the age-old attempts by French troops to invade the Island, and were it not for William Gladstone's intervention, forbidding "any Crown appointed person, judge or member of the army from taking part in any anti-French demonstration",[11] the situation might have escalated. According to Père Rey's research…it seemed that the person behind the trouble was again the Protestant Rector of St. Martin. He even introduced a Bill into the

States to try and ban the Jesuits, but it was heavily defeated on 7 April 1885.[12]

On the whole, their presence was tolerated by most, even though there were a number of incidents including a charge of assault brought to the Police Court in May 1881, and as Eileen Nicolle points out in her comprehensive work *A History of Highlands College*, the reported case of a man who lived next to the former Imperial Hotel (by then re-named Maison Saint-Louis): "... an enraged Protestant, who had lived behind the hotel, said that he would make a half-mile detour whenever he went into town so that he would not have to pass along its walls."[13]

126. - Jersey. - St-HÉLIER. - Vue Générale sur St-Sauveur. - General View on St-Saviours. - E. L.

Maison Saint-Louis with Weather Tower, early 1900s
(Courtesy of Gerard Lecrivain)

By the end of 1881, the Jesuit scholastics and tutors numbered 184, and they were already collaborating closely with the rest of the Catholic community, which had become much more co-ordinated, this almost entirely due to the spirit of leadership brought to Jersey by the Oblates of Mary Immaculate, whom we will be discussing in detail in Chapter 4. The official attitude towards the Jesuits was friendly, and in order to underline the Crown's feelings towards their presence, the

Lt. Governor, General Nicholson, paid a visit to Maison Laint-Louis in 1883:

> This visit was arranged through the good services of Father McCarthy [of the Irish Mission] who had done so much to support the Jesuits in the face of Jersey public opinion, and Mgr John Virtue, bishop of the new diocese of Portsmouth who had once been a naval chaplain and was one of General Nicholson's old friends.[14]

On their side, the Jesuits showed their gratitude to Jersey and the Crown, and for Queen Victoria's Jubilee in June 1887 it was reported in the *Nouvelle Chronique de Jersey* that the whole of the façade of Maison Saint-Louis was illuminated with electric lights, an operation which not only was complex and potentially dangerous in nature, but quite costly. Ten years later, the illuminations were even grander, this time covering most of the major Catholic buildings in St. Helier. It appears that any hostility towards the newcomers was quelled within a few years, by which time most locals realised that their presence might be of benefit to the Island as a whole, and not just to one sector of the community.

Maison Saint-Louis soon became synonymous with theology, philosophy and science. The library itself contained over 200,000 volumes, and the seminary, alongside the Naval College to be built nearby, was the highest establishment of education in the Island.

Notre-Dame-de-Bon-Secours – 1881-1900

In 1856 the French Naval Preparatory School was established at L'Ecole Ste-Geneviève in Paris. Eighteen years later it became known as L'Ecole de Notre-Dame-de-Bon-Secours and was a self-governing school for thirty-four years; at this time it moved from Paris to the naval port of Brest in western Brittany. Notre-Dame-de-Bon-Secours (Our Lady of Good Help) was a Jesuit establishment, and in the same way as the Jesuits from the Scholasticate in Laval who had recently settled into Maison Saint-Louis, the school was affected by the Jules Ferry Laws. The school decided to move to Jersey and continue the students' naval training (obviously solely theory work) on the Island, the aim being to prepare them for entry into the elite Naval College of Brest.

Notre-Dame-de-Bon-Secours (Highlands College)
(Courtesy of Peter Abrams)

The students from Bon Secours and their Jesuit teachers arrived in Jersey in 1881, and not being able to find a suitable building for the college, they settled into villas at Waverley Terrace in St. Helier as well as other lodgings around the town. They soon set up a small chapel at Waverley Terrace too. The school was run from these premises for thirteen years, and by all accounts was an academic success story. In 1884, of the seventy students who gained places at the naval College in Brest, fifteen came from the Jersey school, receiving the top four places in the entrance examinations. As Jean Liouville S.J. reports in his article in *Jersey Church History*, the examiner is said to have retorted to those accusing him of favouritism: "Do you think it's my fault if the Jersey students are good at maths?"[15] It is understood that the high standards achieved in Jersey were largely due to the third year maths teacher at the school, Père Daniel Gras – official statistics indicate that of the 1,586 boys admitted to the Naval College in Brest between 1882 and 1900, more than a fifth had studied in Jersey. Considering that the school did not have its own purpose-built establishment for the first thirteen years, the results were an achievement in themselves, and Bon Secours was praised in writing by one of the most high-ranking admirals.

The fact that academic brilliance, specifically in the field of mathematics and science, had come to Jersey, seemed to prove popular with the Lt. Governor of the Island. The students were no trouble to the Island, and on the contrary, they were bringing with them knowledge, a degree of knowledge that rural Jersey of the late Nineteenth Century badly needed, and as was concluded, this was of benefit to everyone, irrespective of their religious tendencies. A feeling of ever-increasing tolerance was beginning to spread through Jersey, and although a small section of the population did accuse the Bon Secours Jesuits of being a political group exerting too much influence over the young people of Jersey, no major incidents were reported. The Lt. Governor of Jersey visited the school at its Waverley Terrace location in 1883 and was known to be an admirer of their work.

In 1894, the school finally located a building with land which would suit their needs. This was Cardwell House, a large property, formerly used as a private school; it was situated on the grounds of Highlands which quite suitably bordered onto Maison Saint-Louis, thus linking the two Jesuit establishments and increasing the size of the already formidable Holy Hill. A new building was proposed and erected within 27 months. The stone for the building was provided by an open quarry situated on St. Saviour's Road, and the college, designed with distinctive gables resembling upturned ships and anchor motifs along the whole façade, reflected the nature of the college's function. The Chapel was constructed in the central section of the building, and its vault shaped to resemble a reversed ship's hull. The foundation stone was laid in 1895 and the inauguration and blessing took place on Christmas Day 1896. Built by Jersey stonemason and plasterer A. Le Mottée and woodwork experts Messrs Blampied of Oxford Road, the building became the pride and joy of the Jesuit school as well as a feature of the St. Helier skyline.

However, the irony behind the huge efforts and costs required to construct the new school is often overlooked. Within four and a half years of the opening of the new premises at Highlands, Bon Secours Preparatory School was forced to close. Not everyone had been positive about the school's academic brilliance, and jealousy crept in from

Bon Secours College (Highlands), 1907
(Courtesy of Edouard Bosquet)

France itself. Already in 1887, a French deputy had asked the House to exclude all applicants to the Naval College who had done their studies outside the perimeters of the French mainland. This proposal was rejected, but those who felt bitter towards the Jersey school did not give up. Twelve years later, it was suggested that officers for the French Navy "should not be recruited from foreign schools run by Jesuits", nor should they come from a school where the students had learnt "to hate all that smelt of Republicanism".[16] When these frontal accusations failed to have an effect, more devious methods were used, and these ultimately caused the closure of the Jersey naval school. On March 7th 1900, during the vote on the budget, the Naval Minister was asked to modify some rules concerning enrolment locations. These seemed harmless enough, but bureaucracy finally gave the opponents to the Jersey school the answer they had been searching for ever since 1887. The consequences of the proposal meant that Bon Secours Preparatory School would not be eligible for allowing its students to take the entrance examinations, seeing they would not be able to enrol at the French Prefecture of the Department in which they were studying. Overseas locations would therefore be dismissed. This effectively was the death knell for the school, and during the summer of 1900 the school had to be vacated and relocated. By October of that year, the students were transferred to Vannes and Vaugiraud.

Interior of Notre-Dame-de-Bon-Secours Chapel
(Highlands College), 1905
(Courtesy of Edouard Bosquet)

The Observatory

As the whole area became more populated with Catholic scholars, Jersey began to acquire a new reputation; the Jesuits' enthusiasm for learning, in particular philosophy and science, whilst regarded with distrust by some, was welcomed by a growing number of Islanders. Thanks to the academic influx from France, Jersey's status as a centre of culture was being taken quite seriously both on the British mainland and on the continent.

In 1893, Père Marc Dechevrens, a 49-year-old Swiss professor of physics who had taught at the Jesuit colleges of Vannes and Vaugirard, and had played a key role in the development of a major Jesuit Observatory in Shanghai, came to stay at Maison Saint-Louis, mainly for health reasons. His passion for physics and for meteorology soon led him to design plans for an Observatory in Jersey; the Island was an ideal place for studying weather conditions. In addition, an Observatory situated on the grounds of Maison Saint-Louis could only benefit the students who would be well-trained in that field for forthcoming Missions abroad.

Maison Saint-Louis Observatory

Along with another Jesuit at the scholasticate, Père Dechevrens drew up plans for a simple building which would accommodate all their needs. It would consist of a central room, well-lit from above, surrounded by six smaller rooms for living quarters, darkrooms, laboratory, library etc, and would house all the recording instruments needed. The central room would have a flat roof with thick glass slabs supported on a gallery at each corner of which would be secured wind instruments for speed and direction. The design also incorporated a sun recorder, 30 ft off the ground, 170 feet above sea level. The building work was carried out by Samuel Cuzner of 22, Great Union Road, and was completed in September 1894. Whilst designed exclusively for scientific research, one important reminder of its religious origins is clearly visible on the building to this day: on the front stone gable of the building one can still read the lettering IHS, the monogram of the name of Christ adopted by the Jesuits as the symbol of their society, to which they added a cross over the H and three nails under it.

However, Père Dechevrens longed for more than just the Observatory. He had plans to erect a huge metal weather tower, a mini Eiffel Tower, situated well away from surface disturbances and which would calculate and study the wind in greater detail. Père Dechevrens contacted at least four major contractors, both in France and in England. Ultimately, after further correspondence, Père Dechevrens opted for a Belgian engineer named Théophile Seyrig, who worked for the Société Anonyme de Construction et des Ateliers de Willebroeck, in Belgium, and was a former partner of Gustave Eiffel. He became the architect of the Jersey tower.[17] The contract was signed in Paris on April 6th 1894, and arrangements were made for the tower, 50 metres high, to be assembled in segments at the Willebroek works, dismantled and shipped from Antwerp to Jersey.

Work in Jersey commenced in May 1894, and the tower, erected in collaboration with Jersey mason

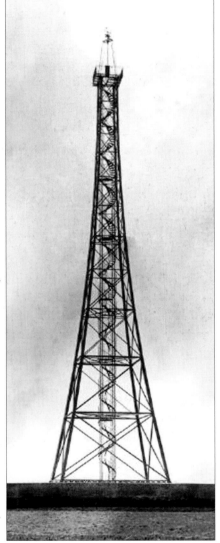

The Weather Tower
(Courtesy of Edouard Bosquet)

Samuel Cuzner, was completed by a Belgian team of metal constructors on November 3rd of that year. The tower was opened and blessed by the Father Rector of Maison Saint-Louis.

The gradual appearance of the huge iron frame attracted the attention of the press, and on October 23rd the *Jersey Express* reported

> Great interest is being manifested in the erection of an observatory which is now being constructed by the Jesuits on their property in St. Saviour's. The tower, which is built of iron, has already reached a great height, from the summit of which a splendid view is obtained, not only of the town but also of the country. It is stated that when the observatory is completed it will be possible to see what is taking place in the armoury of Fort Regent. Should the observatory be opened to public inspection we doubt not that many will eagerly embrace the opportunity of witnessing an indescribable *coup d'oeil* which must well repay any difficulty incidental thereto.[18]

Père Dechevrens did not wait until the completion of the works to begin his meteorological research – the first weather reports published are dated January 1st 1894. However, once the building of the Observatory and tower was completed, a new scientific era was dawning on the Island – state of the art weather calculations and instruments, a unique patented invention by Père Dechevrens known as the Campylograph, and publications of Jersey research at the Office Météorologique National de Paris were just a few of the achievements recorded during Père Dechevrens' lifetime. At this particular stage, these were golden years for the Observatory and tower – and consequently Catholic life in the Island.

4   Les Missionnaires Oblats de Marie Immaculée

Evangelizare Pauperibus Misit Me[1]

In 1880, Mgr James Danell, the Bishop of Southwark, took a decision which was to play a decisive role in the development of Catholic life in Jersey. Aware of the need for leadership and teamwork in the Island, he called upon a French missionary order which had a base in London. These were *Les Missionnaires Oblats de Marie Immaculée* – The Missionary Oblates of Mary Immaculate – and on October 30th that year, a French priest, Père Victor Fick, accompanied by the London Provincial Father Robert Cooke, arrived in St. Helier.

The origins of the Oblates of Mary Immaculate had a background which in many respects mirrored the plight of those Catholics who had fled to Jersey during the French Revolution. Their founder, Charles-Joseph-Eugène de Mazenod, was born on August 1st 1782 in Aix-en-Provence, and as a child of minor noble extraction, found himself thrust into Italian exile in order to escape the Revolution. Political refugees for eleven years, the family was finally allowed back in France in 1802, but by that time, the young de Mazenod had witnessed the breakdown of his parents' marriage, tasted wealth and destitution, and after a period of hesitation, decided to become a priest. His decision stemmed mainly from a desire to help the poor. His return to France in 1802 had been an eye-opener – the French Revolution had left the Church in a state of ruin, many members of the clergy had either opted for the new *modus operandi* of the government or had drifted into unrealistic daydreams of past grandeur, paying little or no attention to the needs of the lower classes. On December 21, 1811, he was ordained a priest in Amiens.

On his return to Aix-en-Provence, he did not take up a regular parish appointment; he decided to assist those he felt needed it most – poor, illiterate country villagers. Eugène soon had a following of other like-minded priests, and they went about preaching in Provençal, the language of the common people, rather than in "educated" French. They called themselves Missionaries of Provence. Ultimately, he and his group took the bold step of going directly to the Pope and asked that they be recognized officially as a religious congregation. His faith and persistence paid off, and on February 17th 1826, Pope Leo XII endorsed the new congregation, the Oblates of Mary Immaculate. The adopted as their motto the Latin *Evangelizare Pauperibus Misit Me* – (He sent me to Evangelise the Poor). Eugène de Mazenod ultimately became Bishop of Marseilles.

Although he had founded the order principally to assist the needy French, he realized that his work could be expanded abroad in the form of missions. In 1841, the first Oblate foundation was established on British soil, and by the time Eugène de Mazenod died in 1861, there were 60 Oblates in Britain. In 1856, Father Robert Cooke had helped set up the first Irish Oblate foundation, and he was the man who also travelled to Jersey on October 30th 1880 along with Père Victor Fick to set up the first Oblate mission in the Island.

The timing of this operation was beneficial to both the Oblates and the Jersey Catholics who badly needed guidance. 1880 was a year of religious turmoil in France, many orders being forced to disband. The anti-clericalism affected the Oblates too, and they were obliged to flee the Sacré Cœur Scholasticate in Autun on November 4, 1880. This ultimately led to the founding of their new International Scholasticate in Rome, but it also meant that many priests were sent elsewhere. Many of the Autun Oblates were first relocated to Inchicore in Ireland. Others, from the Oblate houses of Rennes and Limoges, were sent to Jersey to assist Père Fick in Jersey, a move that was approved by the Superior General of the Oblates, Père Joseph Fabre.

Père Victor Fick, born in Metz in 1845, was ordained Oblate priest in 1872, and had been working in England until his arrival in Jersey. Father Robert Cooke helped Père Fick settle into the presbytery in New Street, then returned to London. Within two weeks he was joined by two more priests, Père F. Guiller and Père Victor Bourde who had both fled Limoges. They soon set up the *Cercle Catholique de St-Thomas*, a social club for the Parish which enabled local Catholics to have a place of relaxation after work. Père Bourde, the former Superior at Limoges, became Rector of St. Thomas'.

Within a short period of time, the Catholic communities settling in Jersey around 1880 – the Laval Jesuits at Maison Saint-Louis and the naval students of Bon Secours, began to mingle with each other, the Jesuits immediately making contact with the like-minded *Dames de Saint-André* at their convent in David Place and celebrating their first Mass in the chapel there. The interaction between the orders was strong, the Oblates actually strengthening the bonds through organised excursions, parish involvement, fêtes, bazaars, recruitment of new parishioners and community spirit. Looking through historical notes and records one can find a common message: the Oblates were becoming the driving force of the Catholic community.

The following two years were used to great effect, and by 1882, Mgr Virtue, the newly-appointed Bishop of Portsmouth,[2] conscious of the fact that the country parishes had lost their initial momentum, asked the Oblates to take charge of St. Matthew's, where Père Volkeryck's successor, Père Matthieu Morin was struggling to keep the church running. Père Morin left on August 5th 1882. By this time, more priests had arrived in St. Thomas' parish, so Père Bourde and Père Guiller moved to St. Matthew's.

Growth at St. Matthew's

The Oblates soon re-established regular church services and activities, the school was re-activated and Père Bourde became acting headmaster, counselling an Oblate Brother he had appointed there as well as others who helped out there. Before long, the Oblates asked the *Dames de Saint-André* to become actively involved in the school, in particular with regards to the education of girls. They accepted and moved into the school.

In April 1884, the *Dames'* Superior in Belgium, Mère Lucie, decided to purchase a plot of land adjacent to St. Matthew's Church. Early June that year a large building began to rise, soon to become the Convent of St. Matthew's. Built largely by the French workforce living in the Island, it was a challenging piece of construction work, and the building was nowhere near ready for the end of the school holidays;

however, the Oblates insisted the school should open, so the *Dames de Saint-André* started the school year on September 9th 1884 living on the premises of the presbytery and accepting a mixed school on a temporary basis until the convent was completed. It was understood that the boys' education would then be supervised by the Oblates and a couple of the Brothers from town. Père Guiller rented a room for himself in a neighbouring house and left the entire presbytery to the sisters and school.

A whole small community therefore left St. Helier on August 29th led by Mère Léonie Slock. The journey was by carriage along a picturesque and varied route, firstly along the sea front; then we entered St. Peter's Valley with its splendid vegetation. On either side there were fuchsia hedges, sturdy geraniums. To the left, the land sloped down to the sea; to the right, rocky crags with chalets and beautiful farms. Leaving the valley the road became steep and finally reached a plateau; there in the distance was a modest spire: we had reached St. Matthew's.[3]

St. Matthew's Convent photographed in 1924
(Courtesy of Mike Edmunds)

Their Superior at the new school was Mother Patricia MacCarthy; she had already played a key role in town at the Anglo-Irish school. Père Bourde, Rector of St. Thomas', was able to report back positively to his Superior General; only a month after the arrival of the *Dames de Saint-André* he noted the transformation within the classes – as he wrote to Père Fabre, just a matter of four weeks earlier the pupils had been like "savages – jumping over benches, hiding under tables, fighting each other..." and now:

> I would like you to see the girls at St. Matthew's. You would weep for joy. There are eighty-eight docile and placid children, soaking up religious instruction, a sight that would make the angels rejoice. What a result, when you consider the nuns have only been there four weeks. And to think that the most obedient of the lot are the bigger boys![4]

Mgr Virtue of Portsmouth wrote to him and commented on the "wonderful" developments in Jersey. As the records of the *Dames de Saint-André* indicate with a certain degree of humour, Père Bourde had good reason to be astonished by the boys' progress in particular. After all, *he* was the one who had attempted to act as headmaster at the school before the arrival of the nuns! In one particular letter to the Sisters, in which he had lamented the lack of discipline within the school, and begged the nuns to come and teach there, he had actually signed off as "Bourde, *policeman* à St-Matthieu".[5] By whatever means the Sisters established discipline amongst the unruliest of the children, the results were impressive. In fact, the Saint-André records report the cases of boys actually dreading the moment when the convent building would be completed and they would have to revert to having lessons with one of the Brothers. One boy's letter to Mother Patricia reads as follows: "Mother Superior, when you have moved into the new convent, please take us with you and leave the girls with the Brother!"[6]

By the end of August 1885 the building of the convent was still not finished, but the Sisters decided they would move into the partly-finished building after all. It was also during the latter part of 1885 that two new Oblate priests took charge of the church, these being Père E. Rolland and then Père Keul.

One Sunday, much to the stupefaction of the workmen present at Mass, the vicar announced from his pulpit that classes would begin in the new building on Monday, September 7th. On the 3rd, they moved into the building which was still full of workers; there wasn't a single lock and key in the place. Thankfully they knew they were living in a land populated by good people where burglars were unheard of, and that God would protect their sleep. On the said day, the girls arrived joyfully, proud of their new school; classes sometimes took place with the occasional workman present, and more than once they were quite keen to interrupt their work to catch a few minutes of the lesson.[7]

As from September 1885 the older boys were taught by one of the Brothers in the old school building, and the Sisters took charge of a mixed class of under-eights as well as girls of all ages. By 1887, the school opened a fee-paying section for the children of wealthy parents as well as boarding facilities. In the meantime, the building work was completed, and the chapel was officially opened within the convent. The chapel, situated on the first floor, was of simple, but unusual design: entirely tiled in white it was almost square in shape and featured a symmetrical high domed ceiling and three windows on the front façade of the building. Above the altar in gold lettering on a red background was the Latin wording *Adveniat Regnum tuum* – (Thy Kingdom Come). On the front façade of the outside of the building a large insignia was carved into the brickwork directly above the chapel, this depicting the entwined crowned letters M and R (*Maria Regina*, Queen Mary) and the words "Immaculate Conception" in abbreviated Latin.[8]

As well as the school, the Sisters established a number of congregations, including the Congregation of the Holy Virgin, the Brotherhood of Our Lady of the Rosary, Our Lady of Mount Carmel as well as the Apostleship of Prayer, the last of which was set up in the Parish on January 19th 1890. All of these initiatives helped a community spirit to flourish and, according to records, the booming Catholic community of St. Matthew's also became the envy of three neighbouring Methodist congregations who apparently had prayed for them to convert to *their* faith!

In February 1886 the new Oblate priest called in to take charge of St. Matthew's Parish was Père Constant Le Vacon. Often referred to by English-speakers as "the right man in the right place",[9] he undertook major refurbishment projects within the Parish grounds, adding an extension to the presbytery and also commissioning a large Breton granite wayside cross to be erected in the church graveyard. This cross, erected in 1889, towers over the cemetery, and was carved by Yves Hernot II of Lannion, a well-known sculptor who produced other pieces of work for the Catholics in Jersey. The graveyard itself houses a number of Oblates and Sisters who died in the Parish; the first to be interred was the Superior of the convent, Mother Patricia MacCarthy, who died on February 8th 1891.

St. Anne's Chapel-School in St. Ouen (Courtesy of Mike Edmunds)

St. Ouen and St. John

It was also Père Le Vacon who sensed the need for further chapels and schools in the west of the Island; and aware of the successful teamwork between the Oblates and the *Dames de Saint-André*, he decided to set up a centre in the westernmost area of Jersey, St. Ouen.[10] He purchased land in the Le Marais area of St. Ouen intending to build a chapel-school; in the meantime, a property called Vanilla House in La Route de Trodez was used as a chapel-school which was opened in 1895 with a Mass taken by Père Alain Mao. The *Dames de Saint-André* sent a nun to the school during the week, and then transformed the building into a chapel, dedicated to St. Anne, for Mass on Sundays. Much later, in 1906, the land at Le Marais was developed and a large granite building was erected. Records indicate that local St. Ouen farmers helped build it and transported over 300 loads of stone in their own carts. Shortly before Père Le Vacon acquired the land in St. Ouen, he had purchased another plot in St. John, at Hautes Croix, in view of building a chapel and school there. It was the *Dames de Saint-André* who built the chapel-school. The first Mass was held at Hautes-Croix Chapel in 1896, and was taken by Père Jérôme Trévien, who was Père Le Vacon's temporary successor. During the four years Père Trévien was in charge of St. Matthew's Parish, he continued to uphold the legacy of his predecessors, and on December 11th, acquired a small bell for the church, Madeleine-Geneviève-Denise; this bell which dated from 1876 had formerly hung at the original Sacré Cœur Chapel at Montmartre in Paris, and was now a gift from Père J.B. Lemius O.M.I. of Paris.[11]

The De La Salle Brothers (1879-1896)

However, not all the operations ran smoothly, and various records indicate areas of disagreement. In 1879, Père Jean François Volkeryck left the Island to be appointed Missionary Rector at St. Joseph's in Dorking, Surrey. In many respects, Père Volkeryck's departure had been a catalyst, one which the priest was probably aware of as he prepared to leave the Island. His presence in Jersey had been overwhelmingly positive, but that of his successor, Père Matthieu Morin, was not. Père Volkeryck, conscious of the fact that the Island needed a much larger network of leaders to bring to fruition the work he had started, left Jersey at a critical time, and his successor's shortcomings led to a more speedy cry for help than may have been the case had he chosen to stay on. Père Morin did not have the drive or the motivation of his predecessor. Parishioners in St. Matthew's were disgruntled; those in town missed their dynamic priest. Other orders were dissatisfied. This was specifically the case of the De La Salle Brothers. Whilst Père Volkeryck had promised them their house, school, furnishings and maintenance of the community, Père Morin announced this could not continue. As a result he suggested the number of Brothers should be reduced from five to three, and proposed a grant of only 2000 francs per year. Thankfully for the De La Salle Brothers, a transfer from the English Province to the Province of Quimper enabled them to overcome these problems, and by 1881, the number of pupils began to rise again. Under the Oblates, a certain degree of stability was maintained until April 1883 when friction between the Brothers and the Oblates was reported. The Oblates were keen to open a school for boys at St. Matthew's, and asked for two De La Salle Brothers to be sent to teach there. The conditions did not meet the Brothers' requirements – they had insufficient Brothers available to achieve this, and as the Oblates could not provide the Brothers with on-site accommodation, they declined. By July 1886 the situation had become fraught; the subsidy from St. Thomas' Parish was reduced even further. A bureaucratic disagreement regarding fee-paying pupils was the last straw for the Brothers, and they threatened to withdraw from Jersey by September 1889.

After much debating, the Brothers' terms were met, and a better school building was found for them. In 1883, the Church had purchased Berry House, a large building situated at Val Plaisant.[12] In 1890 this house was refurbished and expanded, and on June 28th of that year an agreement was signed between the Oblates' Provincial, Père Laurent-Achille Rey,[13] and the Superior General of the De La Salle Brothers, Br Joseph. Peace was established. The school was moved into Berry House, and for the next few years it prospered. A club was set up for Old Boys and was run by one of the priests from St. Thomas'. Interestingly, records from 1889 indicate that the schools at Berry House and St. André's Convent were the only two Catholic Schools in Jersey to be recognised as fully efficient by Her Majesty's Inspector, Mr. Burrows.

However, the concord between the Oblates and the Brothers did not last long. On May 16th 1896, Père Le Vacon, Superior of St. Thomas' Church, informed the Brothers that the agreement they had signed on June 28th 1890 could no longer be upheld. Furthermore, his intentions were to open even more country schools, these to be run by one Brother apiece. As the De La Salle Brothers could not accept these terms, they decided to leave Jersey in July 1896. The conditions stipulated by the Oblates were met by the Brothers of Christian Instruction of Ploërmel who had arrived in Jersey for the same political reasons as all the other orders, and they took over the running of Berry House as well as various country schools.

The Oblates move East

In spite of difficulties and the occasional lack of judgement regarding diplomatic relations within the Catholic community, the Oblates were achieving their goals. The successful interaction at St. Matthew's between the Oblates and the *Dames de Saint-André* led to further developments; the Oblates decided they would take charge at Our Lady of St. Martin's; Père Joseph Guiramand, the founder of the church, had died in September 1881 after having served the Parish for 25 years; his successor, Père C. Tardivon from the Diocese of Nevers, was an ailing man, and he died within two years of taking up his post.[14] At this point, the church was beginning to lose its congregation, so until the takeover by the Oblates, the parish was served by Jesuit Fathers from Maison Saint-Louis. In September 1884, Père Bourde was able to take charge, appointing Père Pierre-Henri Larose O.M.I. to Our Lady of St. Martin on his arrival in Jersey on November 23rd that year. It was clear the Parish would also need a new school, but without help, the Oblates felt this would be a hard task. Moreover, most of the local children were now attending Protestant schools in the east of Jersey. Père Fick, undeterred, obtained the services of a lay teacher from town – one of the Children of Mary; she agreed to come and teach nursery-school children in the tiny sacristy, and the opening date was set for Monday December 1st 1884. To the satisfaction of all concerned, those who started to attend the new school were not just toddlers, but older boys aged between 8 and 12. Before long, the class had reached 40 children, and once again the Oblates were obliged to call upon the *Dames de Saint-André* who sent over one of their teachers from town; the school then moved out of the sacristy and into the presbytery; Père Larose took up lodgings in a neighbouring house which the nuns had managed to rent. The school thrived for over four years with approximately 80 pupils. In 1890 problems arose: the secular teachers were forced to return to town, and this left the boys with an Oblate Brother while the girls were sent back to the Protestant schools.

The *Dames de Saint-André* were swift to react. They had initially agreed to take over from the lay teachers in 1891, but with the future of the school in jeopardy, they decided to bring forward the agreed date, and they moved a group of nuns into the Parish within weeks. The Oblate priest in charge expanded the school on the premises and located a small cottage nearby for the three Sisters. Yet not everyone was satisfied. As is explained in the rather colourful records of the Sisters, an incident was reported at the inauguration service. Apparently, the St. Martin's parishioners, "not always the easiest of folk to handle",[15] became quite aggravated that within a matter of years, their favourite priest, Père Larose, "the eloquent man with the demeanour of an emperor",[16] had been replaced by others they did not relate to as well – firstly Père J.P.M. Féat, then Father H.J. Colin. It is understood Père Fick placated the parishioners by offering his own services to the Parish of St. Martin alongside Père Léger Caux's, and the service is said to have been performed with such a sense of hilarity that the whole church erupted with laughter, thus appeasing any ill-feeling.[17] After that episode the Oblates and Sisters did not encounter any further problems with their parishioners. The Sisters went on to built a new school for the girls, one of the last projects their Superior General in Belgium, Mère Lucie, was to achieve before she died.

Père Caux was accountable for further expansion in the Parish. In 1892 he built an upstairs gallery in the church so that the schoolchildren could attend Mass comfortably; and the following year he added an extension to the presbytery, creating enough room to house another priest, this having become a necessity as another mission in the east of the Island had just been opened.

St. Joseph's, Grouville

Père Caux had given the latest project his entire support: a Miss Corbin (later Mrs Fitzgerald) decided to start a small Catholic school in Grouville, and this was opened on August 14th 1893 in a small house called Les Champs. It was also to be used as a chapel on Sundays for those families living in the St. Clements / Grouville area. The first Mass was held the day after the school opened, on August 15th 1893, perfect timing to celebrate Assumption Day. Père Henri Raffier, the assistant priest of St. Martin, became the first priest-in-charge of St. Joseph's.

Within two years the premises had become so cramped that the Oblates decided to expand, and on February 18th 1895 the General

Council of the Oblates allowed them to purchase a field from a Philippe Le Feuvre called Le Clos de l'Ormel, situated opposite Grouville Arsenal. This plot of land was duly purchased on June 29th 1895. Through funding from St. Thomas', a larger school-chapel was built and opened in 1896.

St. Joseph's Church, Grouville (Courtesy of Cecil Rebours)

Expansion in St. Thomas' Parish

The Oblates' most challenging task was to expand their Parish in town and build the new St. Thomas' Church which had long been promised ever since Père Volkeryck, back in the mid 1870s, had become aware of the need for a larger purpose-built edifice. Père Volkeryck had moved away from Jersey in 1879, but not without leaving a powerful legacy. He had foreseen the need for a larger church in town, and had already located a site at Val Plaisant. By the time he left Jersey to move to Dorking, Père Volkeryck had bought the land and collected a deposit of 50,000 francs towards the building of the new church. According to the records of the *Dames de Saint-André*, Père Volkeryck would "go away each year [...] with his 'beggar's bowl', pleading for offerings towards the planned church from his friends in France and Belgium."[18]

Additionally, he would organise fund-raising bazaars, the most spectacular of these being a four-day event at the Lyric Hall every summer, presided over by Mme la Marquise de Montécot, President of the Ladies of Charity, who would travel over especially from Normandy. The legacy did not go unnoticed, and Père Bourde, in his notes, paid homage to Père Volkeryck's "wonderful dedication to the people of Jersey."[19] In other (unpublished) notes, Père Bourde recognised the fortunate position the Oblates had in Jersey, not only acknowledging Père Volkeryck's hard work, but directly thanking all those who made it possible for them to set up the Jersey mission and work towards building the new church:

> Considering what is happening in France and taking into account what might happen there, we would be ill-advised to complain about our lot. After all, we are in a much more fortunate position than those who have been forced out of their homes. Here in Jersey we are at home, and nobody can control us. We are enjoying communal life; our ministry keeps us going; nobody contradicts the way we run the schools and churches [...] We are our own masters and are free. Neither the government nor the Protestant ministers show any hostility towards us.[20]

As far as they could see, the route was clear, and all they needed to find was someone capable of helping them to raise more money and build the new church.

Père Donat Michaux

It was during Père Victor Bourde's Rectorship at St. Thomas's that the priest decided to invite Père Donat Michaux O.M.I. to preach at the First Communion Service on June 4th 1881. In many respects, this was the event which sealed the future of the new church. When Père Michaux saw the size of the present church, the former Anabaptist Albion Chapel in New Street which could barely fit 400 of the 4000 French-speaking Catholics of the Island, he is said to have exclaimed: "What! In a town like St. Helier where error is glaringly spread abroad, where there are decent churches for all denominations, should Catholics be the only ones without a church worthy of their faith and their

God?"[21] Asked to undertake the building of the new church, Père Michaux immediately accepted. Whether he had been invited to First Communion by Père Bourde with this intention in mind is not stated, but Père Michaux's reputation as experienced architect and ambassador for such projects was well-established in France. In addition, he came from the same part of France as Père Fick, which probably indicates they had known each other at an earlier date.

Donat Michaux was born in Metz on April 18th 1821 and was ordained priest in 1845. In March 1860 he became an Oblate. It was in 1870 that he moved to Notre-Dame-de-Sion near Nancy in north-eastern France, and was the driving force behind the restoration of the tower of the sanctuary as well as the founder and builder of a juniorate. His background was perfectly suited to the challenge in Jersey.

He set about collecting further funds to add to those already amassed by Père Volkeryck; although the latter now lived in England, he remained involved with the project and provided Père Michaux with the names of possible benefactors and descendants of wealthy aristocrats who had come to Jersey during the French Revolution. Père Michaux worked hard collecting money; he even managed to arrange for a fund-raising sermon to be preached at the aristocratic Eglise de la Madeleine in Paris, and before too long, he had enough funds to organise the building of the church.

Laying the Foundation Stone at St. Thomas'

The foundation stone was laid by the Bishop of Portsmouth, Mgr Virtue, on September 6th 1883. One unpublished eye-witness account of the day's events mentions the procession to the new ground, led by Mgr Virtue, followed by dignitaries from the Church as well as Père Volkeryck who had travelled over from Dorking especially in order to witness this event. Jersey coins as well as an engraved silver medal bearing the details of the ceremony were interred in what one nowadays would term a time-capsule. It is estimated that over 2000 people were present at the ceremony.

Amongst members of the Jersey public present was Désiré Thomas Holley, great-grandfather of Bernard Holley who dedicated much of his own youth to St. Thomas' Church and above all to St. Thomas' Sports Club.

Laying of Foundation Stone for St. Thomas' Church,
September 6th 1883 (Courtesy of Bernard Holley)

From Dorking, Père Volkeryck had advised Père Michaux to opt for the same architect as for St. André's Convent and St. Matthew's Church, Alfred Frangeul of St. Malo. Père Michaux had chosen a Gothic style for the new "cathedral", as it was to be referred to, and Frangeul's design, involving a thirteenth-century style with nave, aisles, transepts and chapels forming the arms of the Cross, plus a chancel, fitted in perfectly with the priest's own ideas. His desire was to combine French and Jersey workmanship, French and Jersey materials, a fusion of two places and cultures.

Four Years Later

The final cost of building the church was almost three times the amount stated on the initial contract. Apparently, one of the major delays and increases to the cost was caused by the discovery of water directly beneath the foundations. There were other reasons. Church records held at St. Thomas' indicate persistent squabbles between different workmen, and one lengthy and heated correspondence between Alfred Frangeul and Charles Leclercq, the subcontracted woodcarver from Metz, continued until 1895, by which time it is understood that the church itself had paid off its debts.

The church could not be solemnly consecrated until the debts had been cleared, but with most of the work completed by the autumn of 1887 apart from the wooden scaffolding on the tower, it was agreed to open and bless it officially on October 30th of that year; the old chapel in New Street was closed on October 23rd, a date which in itself was of significance; as Père Fick wrote in a letter to his Superior General:

> The week preceding [the opening of the church] must not be forgotten. On Sunday October 23rd we said goodbye to our old chapel. A strange coincidence: the old chapel was opened on October 23rd 1842. Père Volkeryck arrived on October 23rd 1860, and now, on October 23rd 1887 we held our last service, well attended by all.[22]

The day after the closure of the old chapel, everything was moved into the new church – altars, decorations, statues etc. The presbytery was moved to 17, Val Plaisant.

> It is now Saturday, the day before the opening. Everything is ready. Delicate and sure hands have decorated the high altar. The church has been decked with beautiful decorations like a bride going to meet her husband. The Provincial, Père Rey, has been delegated by the Bishop of Portsmouth to bless the church. The opening is fixed for October 30th, a day that will be held doubly dear to us for two reasons, the opening of the new church and the seventh anniversary of our arrival in Jersey.[23]

The night before the opening ceremony, the Island was struck by a

Wooden scaffolding on
St. Thomas' Church, 1887
(Courtesy of Bernard Holley)

violent storm, an event which was recorded by the Oblates, *Dames de Saint-André* and most newspapers. The sheer strength of the gale could have had disastrous consequences. Père Fick saw this as an omen: "The devil must have shaken with rage. He must have understood that the new church meant war, and all hell seemed to rise up against us."[24]

The rose windows were blown in and glass was scattered all over the slabs and pews from other damaged panes. Rain had leaked in. Many of the decorations were ruined. Père Fick reported concern over the stability of the wooden scaffolding on the steeple which could have crashed down onto neighbouring houses. "It was a miracle this did not happen, although everyone thought it would."[25]

The *Dames de Saint-André* also reported the effects of the storm at St. Matthew's. They too used the word miracle when describing the horrific night of October 29th:

> The cyclone was raging on the plateau, and the sound of the incredible high tide as well as that of the hurricane, produced an awesome noise. Between midnight and one in the morning, the nuns who were praying with fervour, felt a violent shaking and heard a terrible cracking sound followed by a massive crash and cries of terror.[26]

It turned out that a huge furnace chimney weighing anything between five and six thousand kilos, had fallen into one of the bedrooms, completely demolishing the furniture as well as the beds where two nuns were sleeping. Two nuns disappeared under the rubble. Père Le

Vacon was able to give them Communion, but they had to wait until daybreak to be dug out – totally unscathed. Another miracle?

The ceremony was able to take place in spite of the damage to the church. Water and broken glass had to be cleared away before the 10.30 am start, and a massive operation was undertaken by all those involved in the arrangements.

A huge crowd arrived at the church for the opening. A procession of 28 choirboys and 24 cantors followed the Cross. Five Jesuits from Maison Saint-Louis followed them; then came the Oblate priests from the Jersey missions, as well as Père Laurent-Achille Rey, the Provincial. After the blessing, Mass was sung by Père Richard, assisted by a Jesuit deacon and sub-deacon from Maison Saint-Louis. Père Michaux praised all the craftsmen and artists who had contributed to the new church, not forgetting the building contractor, Jean-Marie Huchet of Rennes.[27] He spoke of the blue-grey Breton granite for the exterior stonework and the contrasting Jersey pink granite for the flat wall surfaces.[28] He mentioned the interior shafts of stone quarried from Crozannes and Caen, sculpted into deeply fluted piers of stone, crowned with individually-designed floral capitals. He also noted the meticulous work by Jersey sculptor and stonemason Julian Bedane who had created striking features including the Gothic gargoyles. An unpublished eye-witness account reports Père Michaux smiling sadly as he looked at some of the broken windows before praising the glass artists, most of whose work was provided by the firm Emmanuel Champigneulle & Co of Paris and Bar-le-Duc. The nave windows were designed by the renowned glass artist Bastard of Paris. Laurent-Charles Maréchal of Metz created the two-light windows with small roses in the chancel;[29] others, such as the series of aisle-windows depicting saints were by Georges Claudius Lavergne;[30] both of these artists died in 1887.

Five months later, in March 1888, the former chapel in New Street was refurbished by Père Richard and converted into a hall with a stage and billiard room. It now became the new *Cercle Catholique* which, at a later stage in its existence, would become the Playhouse Theatre.

That same year, 1888, also saw the first Corpus Christi procession in Jersey since the Reformation; it was an opportunity for all those orders who had contributed to the Catholic revival over the past years to come forward and join the procession as a team. These included the

Dames de Saint-André, the De La Salle Brothers and the *Auxiliatrices des Ames du Purgatoire*; The Jesuits from Maison Saint-Louis and the Bon Secours Naval students were joined by other groups, less known but well-represented, including the Third Order of St. Francis and the League of the Sacred Heart. The Little Sisters of the Poor were also present. Often overshadowed by those orders more associated with education, The Little Sisters' role in Jersey was (and still is) of significance to Island life.

The Little Sisters of the Poor

The Little Sisters of the Poor became a part of Jersey life in 1886. Their order was founded in 1839 by Jeanne Jugan from Cancale in Brittany, born during the heat of the French Revolution, on October 25th 1792. During the religious repression of the French Revolution, Jeanne's family continued to uphold their Catholic beliefs, and as a child Jeanne became involved with the sisters of the Third Order of the Admirable Mother. Their order had been suppressed by the authorities, but its members continued to teach catechism in secret. The fifth of seven children, Jeanne Jugan worked as a kitchen maid in Cancale; her employer, the Vicountess de la Choue, was a devout Catholic, and the young Jeanne helped her take care of the sick on her estate. It was during her time working for the Vicountess that she received a marriage proposal which she decided to turn down, preferring to offer her life to God. She moved to Saint-Servan in 1817 and devoted her life to helping the ill and aged, working as a nurse and carer.

In 1839, one single episode led her to founding a small group of women devoted to helping the sick and poor; she gave up her own bed to a blind invalid who had knocked on her door. On December 8th 1842, she and a group of friends took vows of obedience and soon became known as the Servants of the Poor. Their work became so active that the Académie Française awarded the Montyon Prize to Sister Jeanne (or Mary of the Cross, as she became known) "for outstanding praiseworthy activity." Even the Freemasons conferred on her a gold medal. She had it melted down to make a chalice.

Jeanne Jugan became their Mother Superior, although this title was taken from her by the priest acting as the Sisters' spiritual moderator. In 1852 she moved into the mother-house, Tour Saint-Joseph, in Saint-

Pern, where she lived and worked in obscurity until her death on August 29th 1879. It is understood that very few realized she was the founder of the order until after her death. She was beatified by Pope John Paul II in 1982.

The first attempt to bring the Little Sisters of the Poor to Jersey was made in February 1880 by Jersey resident Mme Langliet. She had visited their motherhouse and consulted the clergy regarding the possibility of them sending a group of Sisters to the Island. However, this did not materialise. It took another six years before the Little Sisters of the Poor arrived in Jersey. On March 29th 1886, two Little Sisters of the Poor came over from London; a local couple, Mr. and Mrs. Mowbray Laming, who, it is understood, had known Jeanne Jugan herself and had had close contact with the Order in Paris where they lived for a while, realised that much was needed for the sick and elderly in the Island. They contacted the Sisters' Mother House in Saint-Pern and asked the Mother General to send some Sisters to Jersey and set up a new house. After much negotiation, one of the Mothers Assistant General, Mère Thérèse du Bon Pasteur and Sr Marie de St. Cecilia arrived from London. The following day, Sr Sophie de St. Joseph and Sr Henriette came over from St. Malo. Sr Sophie was to become the Superior of the new house. On April 1st, Sr Joseph St. Victoire arrived, and the five of them moved into two rented terraced houses at 10-11 Grosvenor Street. They had a doorway opened between the two houses in order to make the property larger and more amenable. They immediately set up a chapel which was blessed by the Parish Priest, Rev McCarthy. The foundation was placed under the patronage of St. Augustine. Within days of the first two Sisters' arrival, they began to take in sick people; the records reveal that the first resident the Sisters took into their care was Ernestine Dreux who arrived on April 7th 1886. The first male resident was Louis Ferand who arrived on May 10th.

Their establishment rapidly became known over the Island as The Terrace. They were given significant assistance by other orders living in the Island, and the Jesuits from Maison Saint-Louis in particular sent them food and other useful equipment such as a hand cart. The Jesuits came and blessed their house and one of them even acted as their regular chaplain. The records of the Little Sisters inform us of the Jesuits' gift of a horse and cart which enabled the Sisters to collect alms from the market and various farms in the area. Assistance was also given by the French Oblates of Mary Immaculate at St. Thomas'.

Within a year, the Sisters needed a larger building to work from, and with the help of French benefactors they were able to buy a property situated on St. John's Road called Haute Ville. This property, an old town house with extensive gardens situated at the top of Mont Martin, would now allow them to accommodate eight Sisters, two ladies and eighteen men. They moved in on June 2nd 1887. On June 3rd the Parish priest blessed the house and the temporary chapel, and on June 4th, the students of Bon Secours Naval College came and provided the evening meal for all the residents. Their work proved to be such a success that within a few years extensions had to be built to the premises in order to cope with the growing number of residents. In 1890 the Chapel was built and the year after, more rooms were added to the complex. In 1897 they started work on an extension building for male residents as well as a convent for the Sisters. Further expansions took place in 1912 and 1933. Ultimately they were able to take in 34 residents at any one time. [31]

Debts, Death and Renewal

The building work on St. Thomas' steeple was completed in the months following the official opening, although the damage caused by the storm meant further delays; now it was a question of clearing the debts which had mounted. In five years, the cost of the building had risen to 700,000 francs, and Père Michaux himself travelled to France regularly to collect money and donations in spite of the fact that he was becoming more and more infirm since a train accident in 1882 which had badly crushed his legs. It took six years to clear the debt, and finally, on September 5th 1893, the church, *la Cathédrale*, 196ft high, a statement of Gothic and religious renewal, was consecrated by Mgr Virtue of Portsmouth.

Both Père Michaux and Père Fick who had been so instrumental in expanding the Catholic community, were able to attend the ceremony; within two years, both of them were dead. Père Michaux died suddenly on July 24th 1894 whilst praying; Père Fick died a year later after having contracted a contagious illness from an ailing parishioner.

The Limes

Père Michaux left another legacy upon his death: a house he had purchased on his arrival in Jersey in 1882. For a number of years this property, Maison Saint-Marculf, also known amongst locals as The Limes, had housed a small juniorate for mature students and had a chapel of its own. This juniorate was run almost single-handedly by Père Michaux, and after his death, it proved too costly to keep. Within a year of his death, The Limes (which belonged to the Oblates of the Northern Province), was sold to another Catholic order, *Les Filles du Cœur Immaculée de Marie* – The Daughters of the Immaculate Heart of Mary – a diocesan congregation established in 1842 by the Bishop of Rennes. This congregation had its origins in 14th century Rennes when two sisters of noble extraction, Olive and Elizabeth du Verger, decided to care for people who had been struck by the plague. By 1895 when a small group of sisters of this order came to Jersey, they had already opened houses in Vitré, Rennes, Chateaubourg and Rotheneuf near St. Malo. Based at The Limes, the Sisters worked as private nurses in St. Helier and were soon able to take in patients at the house. Within a matter of years, the house needed further development.[32] A number of the Sisters died in Jersey and their grave can be found at Almorah Cemetery.

End of a Century

As the 19th century was nearing its end, the Catholic community in Jersey was beginning to experience its "golden years". Under the leadership of the Oblates, teamwork and community spirit had managed to thrive. Whatever the political situation in France, it did not matter here. No longer exiled, but on a mission in their new adopted home, French Catholics were starting to build a new solid future in Jersey. They were now an integrated part of Island life.

III

A New Century

1900-1939

5 Golden Years

St. Aubin

The new century started with a feeling of optimism and a determination to expand the network of Catholic establishments. On May 18th 1897 a law was passed in the States of Jersey offering subsidies to anyone willing to open an elementary school, this initiative having been taken to encourage the development of primary education. On June 14th that year a second law was passed offering to pay half the cost of the school-buildings' rent and provide a grant of five shillings for every pupil.

The Oblates focused on St. Aubin's, aware that it was also essential to open a chapel in that area. A report from 1895 by Père Le Vacon had already underlined this need, pointing out the fact that a special train would be laid on every Sunday morning for Catholics living in the Beaumont and St. Aubin's area to take them to St. Helier for Mass at St. Thomas'. So St. Thomas' Parish located a large two-storey house in St. Aubin on Mont les Vaux called Jubilee Hall. A chapel dedicated to the Sacred Heart was opened on Sunday, February 25th 1900 by Père Léon Legrand, Rector of St. Thomas'; this opening ceremony was the first Catholic service in the south-west of the Island for over 300 years. As a gift to the new chapel, the old altar from the original St. Thomas' Chapel (the former Anabaptist Albion Chapel in New Street) which then became the first altar in the *new* St. Thomas' Church at Val Plaisant travelled across the Island and was placed in the Sacré Cœur Chapel in St. Aubin's. In September that year the house opened two classrooms on the ground floor, leaving the top floor entirely free for the chapel. This small primary school enabled families from the south-west of the Island to give their children both primary education and Catholic instruction. Once again, it was the *Dames de Saint-André* who sent a Sister to help out with the school, and reports in the monthly magazine *L'Echo de Saint-Hélier*, published by St. Thomas' Parish, point to a thriving and successful school in St. Aubin. In the May 1901 issue of the periodical, it is claimed the school had 55 pupils and that Her Majesty's Inspector gave the school a glowing report on his visit in December 1900. The chapel too had a good following, and in the May 1901 issue of *L'Echo* the author specifically pays tribute to one generous benefactor who had just donated a statue of the Virgin Mary, although he devotes just as many lines in his article to reprimand those who were not attending Mass on a regular basis, reminding them that these "bad habits" would have to be curbed!

Gorey

Père Jérôme Trévien, Rector of St. Martin's Parish between 1899 and 1906, who had already helped build a larger school for boys at St. Martin in 1902, decided to open a chapel in Gorey in November 1903. At this time, Gorey was also a major holiday destination for French visitors, and he realised the potential a Mass centre could have in the easternmost village of the Island. This chapel, named Our Lady of the Assumption, was so small that by 1908, when Père Louis Gullient was Rector of St. Martin's, a plot of land was bought in Gorey Village and a slightly larger chapel built in 1909. No school was opened at this centre.

The Sacré Cœur Orphanage

In the meantime, Père Léon Legrand, Rector of St. Thomas' and Superior of the Oblates in Jersey since August 30th 1899, was aware of the fact that many poorer parents, both mother and father, needed to go out and work each day and could not afford a nanny. It was also obvious that there was a considerable number of Catholic orphans in Jersey, and that they too needed care. He felt it would be appropriate to establish a Catholic-run house for daycare, and also fund an orphanage. Forty-six year-old Père Legrand, who had previously served in the northern provinces of France, had a sister, Maria, who was Superior General of *La Sainte Famille d'Amiens* (the Holy Family of Amiens), an educational, nursing and missionary order originally

Fig. 1, Right: Monstrance at Our Lady Church, St. Martin. A gift from Emperor Napoleon III

Fig. 2, Below: The Rose Window by Edouard Didron at Beaulieu Chapel (1893)

Fig. 3, St. Thomas' Church in 1904 (Courtesy of Jeanne Moore)

EVANGELIZARE PAUPERIBUS MISIT ME

INRI

PAUPERES EVANGELIZANTUR

O M J

S^{TE} FAMILLE S^T AMIENS

Fig. 4, Above: Detail of stained glass window at Sacré Cœur Chapel by Augustin Burlet. Tribute to Oblats de Marie Immaculée and La Sainte Famille d'Amiens

Fig. 5, Right: Detail of stained glass window at Sacré Cœur Chapel by Augustin Burlet

Fig. 6, Memorial Stone at Highlands College on the site of the former Bon Secours Cemetery

founded in Besançon by Jeanne-Claude Jacoulet in 1803. Mère Jacoulet, as she became known, was born in 1772, and had witnessed the anticlericalism of the French Revolution; in 1798 she decided to open some small village schools in order to bring back the element of faith to poorer children's education. Her project proved to be a success, and in 1803 she founded a congregation, *l'Association Sainte Famille*. By 1817, her missionary work had spread beyond Besançon, and she was asked by the Bishop of Amiens to open a school there. At her death in 1836, her congregation had opened houses in Bourges and Nevers, and was going from strength to strength.

When Père Legrand decided to contact his sister in Amiens, he knew that if his plan to open an orphanage and crèche in Jersey should succeed, he would need a team of reliable staff to run them; Maria Legrand promptly agreed to assist her brother by sending two of the Order's Sisters. Additionally, the timing for this new project in Jersey was of benefit to the Sisters in France, as they too were affected by the secularisation of the education system in the country. Since 1900 even more new laws were affecting the country's clerics, and by 1901-02, with the dissolution of religious teaching orders introduced by Emile Combes, followed shortly by the Separation of Church and State in 1905, the *Sainte Famille*'s houses were forced to close. Their property was liquidated. Those from Amiens were fortunate in having the new mission in Jersey, others fled to Belgium. The sisters from Besançon moved to England.

In the December 1900 issue of *L'Echo de Saint-Hélier*, Père Legrand personally announced the imminent inauguration of *La Crèche*, a daycare house for working mothers. This crèche was to be opened the following month in rented accommodation at 31 Portland Place, Midvale Road. On December 5th 1900 Sr Laure Wiart arrived in Jersey with a companion; Père Legrand's sister in Amiens promised her brother that other Sisters would be sent shortly. On January 5th 1901, they began working at Midvale Road, and before long, the place was known familiarly as *La Pouponnière*, the crèche. As well as the daycare house, the establishment opened its doors to orphans needing full-time housing, and this proved to be an even greater success than the nursery which, by May 1901 was facing competition from another co-religious centre. The orphanage, on the other hand, now known as the Sacré Cœur Orphanage, was taking in many children, and within a few months Père Legrand knew he would have to find a much larger property to house everyone comfortably. In the May 1901 issue of *L'Echo*, he said:

> The Sacré Cœur Orphanage is progressing quietly but at such a rate that one could get alarmed were one not reassured that works under the protection of the Sacred Heart are guaranteed success. We have already received fifteen or sixteen orphans; where will it stop? The premises are too small, and those people devoted to the work and who founded it are going to have to make some plans...

Summerland House in 1901 (Courtesy of Sister Peter)

Plans were obviously made rapidly, and within a month, Père Legrand as well as the *Sainte Famille* Sisters located a house with land on the outskirts of town which seemed ideal. The property was known as Summerland House and was situated at Rouge Bouillon, which at that time was a fairly rural suburb of St. Helier. The house, which belonged to a Dr. Le Blancq, was for sale, and the Sisters, with the help of St. Thomas' Parish, and Père Legrand's own inheritance, bought it promptly. They decided to keep the Midvale Road premises for the housing of staff until the Summerland property was developed. As Père Legrand noted in the August 1901 issue of *L'Echo*:

On July 4th the Sacré Cœur Orphanage was transferred to Summerland, Rouge Bouillon. Air and light will be in abundance, the same goes for space! For we shall build! Yes, we must aim to build: this project is developing so fast that the space occupied at present by the children of both the Orphanage and the Crèche will soon be inadequate.

Père Legrand and the *Sainte Famille d'Amiens* started to build a large house adjoining the original Summerland property. This was to be the new orphanage, leaving the main house free for the convent. From *L'Echo* of December 1902 we know that the building was nearing completion, and that the statue of the Sacred Heart was given its blessing on the evening of Sunday November 30th at St. Thomas' Church; the statue, we are informed, was a souvenir from the three-week Mission (organized by Père Legrand) which concluded that same evening:

It was placed in the chancel, in front of the high altar, on a temporary pedestal. It will stay there until its actual pedestal is completed at the Summerland property at Rouge Bouillon. What a joy it will be for the devoted disciples of the Sacré Cœur, to see the statue of their beloved Saviour crowning the orphanage building and stretching his blessing hands over the town, over St. Thomas' Parish, over the entire island!

The Orphanage was a great success. According to the records held by the former Mother Superior of the Orphanage, Sister Peter Gabrielle (who now resides at Clubley Estate, St. Helier with Sisters Ida and Phyllis, both highly active members of *La Sainte Famille d'Amiens*), there were nine Sisters, 78 children and 13 babies living at the Sacré Cœur in December 1904. Most of the children were of primary school age. Approximately fifty young girls and boys would make their way to St. André's Convent each morning, and about twelve older boys would head for St. Thomas' (run by the Brothers of Christian Instruction of

The Sacré Cœur Orphanage and St. Joseph's Juniorate prior to 1926
(Courtesy of Sister Peter)

Orphans and Sisters, early 1900s (Courtesy of Sister Peter)

Père Léon Legrand with two orphans, early 1900s (Courtesy of St. Thomas' Church)

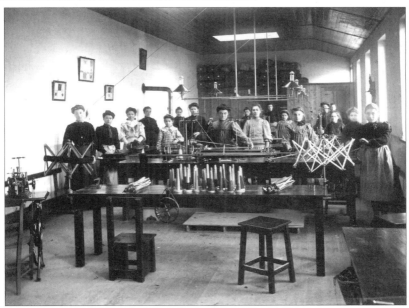

The Summerland Knitwear Factory – Ouvroir du Sacré Cœur, 1908 (Courtesy of Sister Peter)

Ploërmel). From the age of thirteen the boys would start work as apprentices in different trades in town, although many stayed at the Sacré Cœur where they could develop gardening and fruit-growing skills on the vast property. The Orphanage grew in size and stature: Sister Peter's records indicate the admission of over one hundred children in 1907, with 15 Sisters in residence on July 4th that year.

As far as the girls' further education was concerned, another significant step was taken by the Orphanage on September 18th 1905 when a textile factory was opened in an neighbouring building. Initially, girls over the age of thirteen were given lessons in housekeeping. This turned into a College of Domestic Science. Then the *Ouvroir* or workplace was opened, and as from 1905 girls could learn sewing and knitting. A weaving shed was added to the workshop, and as time went by, the factory became a larger business. Père Legrand, who had Oblate contacts in the German-speaking world, managed to arrange the import of special German machinery. In October 1909 the first exhibition of finished textiles was held by the Sisters and girls at the *Ouvroir*. The workshop opened its doors to girls from the Parish and town, and by 1910 there were about sixty young women working there, of which only about ten actually came from the Orphanage. Ultimately, the factory was becoming a steady business, and the Sisters realised that outside help would be needed. The Summerland Knitwear Company was founded by the Sangan family and they took over the running of the factory, although most of the people employed there were either from the Orphanage or from St. Thomas' Parish.

Père Legrand, who was Rector at St. Thomas' until 1911, had further plans regarding expansion within the Island as a whole, and it is understood the Orphanage had close links with farming land in St. Aubin's and also opposite Samarès Manor, where church-funded land was in the process of being turned into a School of Gardening, to be called La Ferme Baudains. However, the school never opened: in 1914 World War I broke out, and all those plans had to be shelved.

In 1912, two years before the outbreak of World War I, part of the Summerland property was turned into a Juniorate, a college for the training of future Oblates. St. Mary's House (Maison Sainte-Marie) was situated on the Roussel Street side of the property, and had been bought by Père Legrand on behalf of the Parish. Until 1912, the house (formerly the Jersey Modern School) was used for the education of

JERSEY - Cour de récréation du Juniorat. A gauche, la salle de récréation et de séances, avec l'aile principale des bâtiments de l'Orphelinat. Au fond et à droite, bâtiments scolaires à l'usage des Junioristes

Students outside St. Joseph's Juniorate, 1920s
(Courtesy of Sister Peter)

Interior of Sacré Cœur Orphanage Chapel built in 1926
(Courtesy of Sister Peter)

older boys. After the expulsion of religious orders in France, the Juniorate initially transferred to Belgium. The Oblates felt they were too far away from Brittany, the most Catholic region of France, so Jersey became the ideal location. When it first opened, St. Joseph's Juniorate at St. Mary's House started out with twenty students. Père Legrand, who had already founded a Juniorate in Holland in 1885, was in charge. He remained in charge until December 8th 1923 when he was appointed Provincial of the Northern French Province. He returned to Jersey in 1926 and resumed his post at the Juniorate on August 15th 1928. All in all, the Juniorate thrived in Jersey for nearly twenty years and finally closed down on July 7th 1931 when conditions in France allowed the Oblates to develop a new Juniorate in Pontmain (Diocese of Laval).

The Orphanage and Summerland property soon became a hub for Catholic life in St. Thomas' Parish. It provided childcare, apprenticeships for both girls and boys, a market garden, a thriving knitwear business, a laundry, a printing press, a bustling student life as well as a meeting point for religious societies. There was even a *Salle des Fêtes*, a dance hall. The grounds were extensive, and they were developed fully, without ever sacrificing the "space, air and light" which Père Legrand had felt was essential to the welfare of children.

In 1925, it was decided to add another annexe to the main house, this time to the left: a much-desired chapel. The foundation stone was laid that year, and over the coming year, the chapel was built. It was blessed and opened by Bishop William Timothy Cotter of Portsmouth on September 20th 1927. Of particular note are the stained-glass windows (which are still in the building, now an office). These windows were created by the famed glass artist from Chalon-sur-Saône, Augustin Burlet, born on April 2nd 1892, who became renowned throughout France for his impressive designs. Active until his death in 1953, he was commissioned to produce glass windows at numerous sites in France, especially in the Lyons area, and in 1985, a major exhibition organised by the Basilique Notre-Dame de Fourvière in Lyons was entirely devoted to his work. The windows at the Sacré Cœur Chapel in Jersey all pay tribute to those who established the Orphanage. One window depicts the Oblates' logo and motto, featured above the wording *Sainte Famille d'Amiens*. Biblical scenes in vivid colours adorn all three major windows.

Orphans and Sisters of the Sainte Famille with Père Legrand, early 1930s
(Courtesy of Sister Peter)

Pre World War II memories of the Orphanage are still to be found amongst a number of Jersey residents. Jean "Jack" Jouanny was born in Jersey to French parents in 1922. Orphaned at an early age, he was placed into the care of the Orphanage, and has clear recollections of the nuns' strictness. "They weren't too happy with us when the boys decided to take a peek on the girls' side of the Orphanage", he joked, explaining that the house's living quarters were divided into one section for boys and another for the girls. He also recalls the weekend tasks he was asked to do by the Sisters. These involved pumping the bellows of the organ at St. Thomas' Church or delivering fruit and vegetables from the Orphanage gardens to the enclosed orders of Carmelite nuns living on "Holy Hill", and in return, collecting the hosts to be taken to the chapel. Other boys were given day jobs as gardeners at Maison Saint-Louis or Bon Secours, where by now the Brothers of Christian Instruction of Ploërmel were settled. One of Jack Jouanny's own brothers worked at The Limes as a gardener for the nursing Sisters. "We all used French as our main language at the Orphanage, some of the nuns couldn't speak much English; besides, we were all French-speakers back in those days", he explained. He too went to the elementary school at St. Thomas', although with regards to his schooling, most of it had to be in English.

Memories evoked by Sister Peter, the former Mother Superior of the Orphanage, are poignant; orphaned at birth in Guernsey, and the youngest of six children, she was sent to the Orphanage at the age of two. After her elementary schooling, she began working at the knitwear factory as a seamstress at the age of 14. It was at this time that she knew her vocation was to become a nun. She also felt a need to improve conditions at the Orphanage, which in her opinion had remained too Victorian for the times. A rebel and reformer at heart, she had lacked motherly affection while growing up at the Orphanage, and it was her desire to revitalise the running of the Orphanage and give the young children a more loving upbringing. She worked at the knitwear factory until after World War II, at which stage she studied to become a nun in Amiens, before ultimately returning to Jersey in order to fulfil her personal pledge and transform the Orphanage's Victorian approach to child-raising.

Boy Confirmants outside the Orphanage including the young Philip Le Troquer, future Head Gardener
(Courtesy of Andrée Etienne)

One of the most well-known Jerseymen who attended the Orphanage and later worked there for over sixty years, was Philip Le Troquer. Born in St. Martin in 1896, his parents died when he was a child. At the age of nine, he entered the Orphanage along with his sisters and brothers. As he recalled in a "Personal View" interview, life was "nice but disciplined" at the Sacré Coeur. His daytime routine would involve a church service first thing in the morning, breakfast, and then school by 9 o'clock. He went to St Thomas' School but ate all three meals at the Orphanage. After school he would do his homework and then do some cleaning on a rota basis. Once a quarter he would be allowed out alone as long as he came back to the Orphanage by 6pm. He would usually visit his uncle. His aunt lived in St Aubin and he would visit her once a year. He left school at 13 and he decided he wanted to become a gardener, taking lessons with Mr Nouvel at Bon Secours College every evening throughout the winter. After fours years training he was awarded a certificate, and had hoped to start working full-time as a gardener at the Sacré Cœur. However, the World War I had broken out and within weeks he was mobilised and drafted to India. On his return to Jersey one of the first people he visited was Père Legrand "who was like a father to me." He ultimately became Head Gardener at the Orphanage and retired at the age of 88. Philip Le Troquer died in 1986.

Bells and Organ at St. Thomas' Church

Back in 1904, further changes and developments were taking place at the "Cathedral". To celebrate the 25th Jubilee of Père Legrand's priesthood, funds were collected from parishioners, and a bell named Maria Immaculata (20 cwt, 4E) was given to St. Thomas's Church. This bell, cast by Paccard of Annecy, was rung for the first time on December 8th 1904 and blessed that same day by Mgr Émile Jean Baptiste Marie Grouard, Vicar Apostolic of Athabaska in Canada where the Oblates had established missions.

In 1905, Père Legrand acquired an organ for St. Thomas' Church – this organ came from the sanctuary of Notre-Dame des Lumières in Avignon, one of the first properties bought by Eugène de Mazenod for his missionaries in 1837; the Oblates had to leave the seminary due to the dissolution of religious orders in France.

*"Maria Immaculata" Bell at
St. Thomas' Church, 1904
(Courtesy of Bernard Holley)*

Sₜ «Maria Immaculata» Bell of St Thomas Church, Jersey.
Rung for first time December 8ᵗʰ 1904.

Eight years later, in 1913, Père Gullient, then Rector of St. Thomas', was given two new bells for the belfry - these were Eloise-Ida-Thérèse de l'Enfant Jésus (5 cwt, Treble B) and Jeanne-Eliane (10 cwt, 2G Sharp). Both of these bells were cast by Cornille-Havard of Villedieu-les-Poêles in Normandy, and were blessed by Mgr Henri Delalle, Vicar Apostolic of Natal in Africa. In 1915, a white marble monument to the memory of Père Michaux, the founder of the church, was installed.

A fourth bell was given to the church in 1929: Père Mao, Rector of St. Thomas' accepted the bell which was presented to Père Legrand on the occasion of the Fiftieth Jubilee of his priesthood; the gift of this bell was also a tribute to Père Legrand's work at Summerland. The bell, Clotilde Louise Léonie (16 cwt, 3 F Sharp) was cast by Paccard. The traditional benediction service, which resembled a baptism ceremony, involved the bell having "godparents", and in the case of this bell its godparents were Louis Sangan (representing the knitwear factory) and Mother Marie Clotilde (Superior General of the *Sainte Famille d'Amiens*). A few people still have memories of this particular ceremony – these include Jerseywoman Mrs Andrée Etienne (daughter of Philip Le Troquer), who was a child at the time: she was most impressed by the *dragées* (French sugar-coated almonds traditionally given at babies' baptisms) which the children in attendance were given.

The fifth and final bell received at St. Thomas' was Anne-Marie-Andrée-Ignace, known familiarly as *Le Bourdon* – the Great Bell or Bumblebee. This bell (52 cwt, Tenor B), cast by Paccard, was received in 1937 by Père Théodule Maré.

Interior of St. Thomas' Church, 1904
(Courtesy of Jeanne Moore)

The Corpus Christi and the role of the *Suisse*

The records at St. Thomas' Church do not tell us precisely when the old French tradition of the *Suisse* was introduced in Jersey, although there are some indications that there was a presence of a uniformed man leading the first Corpus Christi procession at the church in 1888. However, we know for certain that it was during the early twentieth century that the custom of having a *Suisse*, a leader of processions, both for Mass on Sundays and for more formal events such as Corpus Christi, was established at the church. St. Thomas' Church, known throughout the Island as the French Cathedral, was deemed worthy of this status. The tradition of having a *Suisse* in large cathedrals in France originated as a result of the *Garde Suisse* troops deployed by French kings (Louis XIII-Louis XVI) and the *Cent-Suisses*, a regiment created by Charles VIII which was integrated into the king's guard, most of whom were massacred at the height of the French Revolution on August 10th 1792 defending the monarchy outside the Tuileries in Paris. As from the 17th Century in France, large mansions or the houses of nobles would have a Suisse in uniform working as concierge or porter. Churches and cathedrals of importance also incorporated a uniformed layman into their services; he was neither a sexton nor a verger nor a beadle, but a man who would cover many of these duties whilst maintaining a unique role of his own. Dressed in a dark blue or red uniform and wearing a bicorn hat, he would lead the procession into the church bearing a halberd in his right hand and a silver-topped staff in his left. This tradition also has emblematic roots at the Vatican, the Pope's own Swiss Guard, and it is thought that symbolically, a *Suisse* in French cathedrals acted as a reminder of the papal guard.

The *Suisse* in Jersey had two uniforms – a red one for Mass on Sundays, and a dark blue one for more formal occasions. Both of these uniforms along with the halberd have been preserved in Jersey and are now the property of the Heritage Trust, and judging from the fabric, stitching and style, one can ascertain that these uniforms were both made during late Victorian times. It would appear they were both made in France. Attention to detail has been meticulous – the jacket buttons depict cherub faces and sunrays, reminding one of a monstrance. The sashes are both red; one bears the entwined initials ST in gold thread (referring to St. Thomas), the other has the initials OMJ (for which one reads OMI - Oblates of Mary Immaculate). The halberd's head is

*The Suisse, Jean-Marie-François Le Fondré, leading a
pre-Second World War Corpus Christi Procession
(Courtesy of St. Thomas' Church)*

a meticulous piece of metalwork, incorporating the entwined initials A and M, a traditional monogram for the Virgin Mary – a shortened form of *Auspice Maria* (Under the Protection of Mary).

Although it is unclear when the *Suisse* first took up his role at St. Thomas' Church, it is known that there have only ever been three *Suisses* working for the Parish; faded photographs from the early twentieth century depict an elderly man bearing the halberd and staff and leading altar boys into the church. His identity is not known for certain, although some sources have suggested his name was Lefevre. The second *Suisse* took up his role in the late 1920s: he was Jean-Marie-François Le Fondré (1879-1965), and it was he who led the very first Corpus Christi procession which actually involved parading through the streets of St. Helier on June 22nd 1930. Although there had been Corpus Christi celebrations in Jersey since 1888, this was the first for 372 years which involved a complete traditional procession through the town; every newspaper on the Island reported the day's events.

The *Suisse*, Mr Le Fondré, led the parade followed by one Cross-bearer and two acolytes, and after them came over twenty-five different orders, groups, bands and choirs walking four abreast, with Père Alain Mao carrying the Blessed Sacrament under a canopy borne by four Jesuits. The *Jersey Morning News* reported that "Despite the adverse weather conditions, over 8000 Roman Catholics took their places in the procession, JMT buses being run from all parts of the Island to enable the country people to attend." The procession started at 3pm that afternoon at St. Mary's and St. Peter's, Vauxhall, "and the line extended from David Place to Rouge Bouillon." The route proceeded along David Place, Midvale Road, Rouge Bouillon to Roussel Street and ended at St. Mary's House. We are told twenty-six priests were in attendance and that 14 flower-strewers immediately preceded the Canopy. A three-tiered altar was situated near the door of St. Mary's House, and the huge square was filled with the crowd. Benediction was given by Père Legrand, and the choir from Maison Saint-Louis rendered various pieces in Latin. Returning back to town along Rouge Bouillon, Great Union Road and Windsor Road, the procession arrived at St. Thomas' Church, the Blessed Sacrament carried this time by the Father Rector of the Jesuits. The ceremony closed with a benediction by Canon John Hourigan and a hymn to the Pope. "St. Thomas' Church was crowded to its utmost capacity and the procession lined the steps and extended into Victoria Street."

Corpus Christi Celebrations at the Sacré Cœur, 1930s
(Courtesy of Sister Peter)

The Corpus Christi of 1931 was even larger than the year before, and newspaper reports suggest that ten thousand people attended it. This led to a number of poignant questions which were raised in the press regarding the status of the Roman Catholic Church in Jersey, and even ardent Protestant sources had to admit that the Catholic Church had attained record numbers of followers and was without doubt the most dynamic faith in the Island. The heading of a leader article by the Protestant editor of the *Jersey Critic* on June 13th 1931 asked directly: "Is Jersey Becoming Roman Catholic?" It continued:

I am not quite sure that there were ten thousand people in that procession on Sunday; probably the number was nearer eight thousand. But of this I am sure – that everybody in that procession goes to church, possibly not every Sunday, but certainly with some degree of regularity. And – this is the staggering fact – it cannot be said of either the Anglican church or the Nonconformist connexion that either has eight thousand worshippers, regular or otherwise. The greater part of the people in Jersey who call themselves Protestants never see the inside of a place of worship except at weddings or funerals, and of all the Protestant churches and chapels only a few are well attended. In the meantime the comparatively small number of Roman Catholic churches are filled every Sunday with devout congregations.

For a number of years now the Roman Catholics have been carrying out in the Island a policy of peaceful penetration. They have done their work quietly, but they have done it thoroughly and consistently. The average Roman Catholic priest works far harder for much less money than the average Anglican minister. Like the vicar of Wakefield, he is "passing rich on forty pounds a year." He is entirely devoted to his Church and keeps a watchful eye on his flock. He visits his people and keeps in close touch with them, his constant aim being to keep them under the discipline of the Church to whose service he has devoted his life. And in this concentration of aim and endeavour we find the answer to the question – "Why is the Roman Catholic Church going ahead in Jersey at such a rate?"

The author of this article had done his research; he knew that the rapid growth of Catholic following in the Island over the past fifty years was largely due to the priests' input. As Père Vincent Igoa O.M.I. points out in his study of the Oblates' years in Jersey:

Even if not inclined to be churchgoers, people were pleased that priests bothered about them. Slowly the congregations filled up the churches and the schools became too small. In 1910 Père Legrand gave figures of the families visited by the Oblates: St. Thomas, 734; St. Aubin, 117; St. Matthew, 270; St. Ouen, 75; St. John, 118; St. Martin, 185; Grouville, 130; Gorey, 29; total = 1658 families regularly visited amounting to around 7000 individuals. This does not represent the total Catholic population of the parishes run by the Oblates, but only the number of those known to the Fathers.

The article in the *Jersey Critic* had voiced the thoughts that many Jersey residents had long been aware of, and the annual popularity of the Corpus Christi procession continued to act as a symbolic reminder that Catholic presence in the Island was strong. Jean-Marie-François Le Fondré continued as *Suisse* until around 1948 when he was replaced by Ferdinand Joseph Lecrivain (1908-1971). An active member of the French section of the Knights of St. Columba, Mr. Lecrivain continued in his predecessor's footsteps, heading the annual Corpus Christi procession, but above all, leading the Mass each Sunday and assisting the priest with various functions during the service; he continued as *Suisse* until his death in 1971 at which point no further *Suisse* was deployed. The principal reasons for this were twofold and will be discussed in greater detail later in this work: major elements within the church service had changed, thus not needing the presence of the *Suisse*; and secondly, the Corpus Christi had ceased to take place – symbolically also underlining the start of an unstoppable decline.

Clubs, Societies and Pilgrimages

One means of securing a feeling of fellowship within the Catholic community in Jersey was the introduction of various clubs, confraternities and associations. Already under Père Volkeryck in the 1870s, a number of groups had been formed, amongst these the Children of Mary, the Ladies of Charity and the Conference of St. Vincent de Paul. Other groups which were established over the years included the Children of St. Louis (for younger girls), the Third Order of St. Francis, the League of the Sacred Heart, the Apostleship of Prayer, the Confraternity of the Propagation of the Faith and the Eucharistic Crusade. The *Cercle Catholique de St. Thomas,* which endured a number of interruptions and fresh starts, went through numerous changes. After having closed and restarted various times in the early 1900s, it re-opened again on December 7th 1908, this time housing the first cinema in Jersey, run by Langlois and Poulain. In 1905 the Catholic Boys Brigade was founded in St. Thomas, St. Matthew and St. Martin, their motto being *Ne cede malis* – "Do not give in to evil". The Catholic Youth was formed in 1908 with rules largely derived from the scout movement, and after the 1914-1918 War, Scout Troops and Cub packs were formed in the three main parishes. Later, a joint company for girls from both St. Thomas' and St. Mary's and St. Peter's was started. In 1919, Père Legrand made an arrangement with the

Superior of the Jesuits at Maison Saint-Louis; this enabled the youth clubs to receive guidance from the Jesuits, and it also enabled a "Patronage" for boys not old enough to join the *Cercle Catholique* to be set up.

143. JERSEY. — St Thomas boys brigade
Brigade St-Thomas

Catholic Boys Brigade outside St. Thomas' School
(Courtesy of Gerard Lecrivain)

Music was also given importance, and a youth band called L'Avenir was formed. This survived until World War II. One of the strongest clubs for young people was the St. Thomas Sports Club, a venture started by Père Pierre Jort who was Rector of St. Thomas between 1926 and 1933. The Sports Club (and Boys' Friendship Club for the younger section) used the premises at St. Mary's House vacated by the students of the Juniorate in 1931. There, they had space for gymnastics training, table tennis, rifle shooting and billiards as well as a canteen and quiet room. The Sports Club had a large following, and according to Bernard Holley, who was Treasurer, then President of the Club in post-war years, many boys would spend hours devoted to training for spectacular displays at the Summer Fête which would take place in the grounds at Summerland. This Fête, which took place on the last Thursday in August each year, was organized by John Etienne for nearly thirty years. The members of the Sports Club were naturally also heavily involved in church activities, and each Easter, Bernard Holley and his team would prepare stunning decorations for St. Thomas' Church.

In 1930, the Knights of St. Columba approached Père Mao, Rector of St. Thomas, and Council 229 was created for Catholic men from St. Thomas, St. Matthew and St. Martin. The Oblates provided the Knights with a meeting room and a chaplain.

One peculiarity which was introduced in Jersey was the "Men's Mass" which was started in 1904. The Parish of St. Thomas had long realised that men were always outnumbered at Mass by women. In 1888 a survey of those who attended the Easter services showed that whilst over 1200 women attended, only 400 men were present. Although the Men's Mass proved popular, it did not alter the situation very radically. A new survey held in 1913 revealed that only 529 men performed their Easter duties compared to the 1135 women.

Another form of religious expression was the pilgrimage. One was started by the Jesuit scholastic Théodore Wibaux from Maison Saint-Louis at the end of the nineteenth century, and St. Matthew's was selected as the pilgrimage centre in honour of the Sacred Heart. His project was approved by his superiors, and a large statue of the Sacred Heart was placed above the High Altar. Every week, scholastics would leave Maison Saint-Louis at 4.30 am and head for St. Matthew's to reach the church in time for the 6 am Mass.

In 1915, the Oblates asked Mgr Cotter, Bishop of Portsmouth, if they could arrange a pilgrimage in honour of St. Helier, and this was granted. Mgr John Henry King, then Secretary to the Bishop, added in his reply: "I am personally delighted to hear you are going to revive the old Catholic ways in the Island."

There was also a yearly pilgrimage to St. Anne's in St. Ouen, on the Sunday closest to July 26th (the Feast of St. Anne). An unpublished diary in French by the Oblate Rectors of St. Matthew's, the *Codex Historicus*, makes annual references to the pilgrimage which would attract crowds from all parishes and even involve minor choirs such as the one from St. Aubin's.

Another pilgrimage was aimed at taking Jersey-based Catholics to Lourdes each year, and the first of these was arranged by Père Gullient on August 30th 1913. A detailed description of each pilgrimage between

1919 and 1950 is also given in the *Codex Historicus*. The 1921 entry starts as follows:

> The Jersey pilgrimage to Lourdes took place on August 19th. Eight of our parishioners took part and joined up with those from St. Thomas'. In all there were 49 pilgrims accompanied by Père Pitard and Père Schmidt. Everyone met up at St. Thomas', where the Rector of St. Thomas', Père Mao, gave us blessings. The bells announced our departure.

Each year, different aspects of the pilgrimage are highlighted by the diarist. Of specific poignancy is the 1939 entry which is tinged with apprehension – everyone knew that the severity of the War was developing rapidly. Led by Père Jean Louis Messager, "it was a troubled pilgrimage; the shadow of war was felt by all. Everyone felt tense, some of the group wanted to cut short the stay in Lourdes." However, in spite of an increasingly fraught atmosphere they decided to stay on for the length of time they had planned; they even made a stop at Pontmain on their return trip, despite the fact that "there were soldiers everywhere." Judging from the diarist's wording, one must assume their decision to stay the full length of the trip was not an act of defiance but one of intrinsic faith: "Those protected by the Holy Virgin are guaranteed safe passage".

6   Holy Hill (ii)

Carmelite Nuns

"Holy Hill" had become a vast Catholic network; Beaulieu and Maison Saint-Louis were impressive landmarks located at either end of the area, flanking the whole of the Highlands perimeter, the Observatory and Mont Millais. The presence of Catholicism in this part of town was powerful, and Catholics coming to Jersey from France were drawn here like a magnet.

As a result of the religious instability in France, the dissolution of religious establishments (followed shortly afterwards by the Separation of Church and State in 1905), three groups of Carmelite nuns moved to Jersey in the late summer of 1901. The Carmelites, an enclosed silent order whose origins extend as far back as the 12th century, were unlike the rest of the orders and groups who came to Jersey seeking refuge, in that they did not seek to become an active part of society; in accordance with the discipline of their order, they came in search of a place where their routine of silence, contemplative prayer and seclusion from the world could be accepted. The Carmel of Tours settled into a townhouse at 4, Westbourne Terrace, a residence situated to the north of a large property known as The Beeches, which would later become De La Salle College.

The Carmelites of Saint-Pair from the Diocese of Coutances moved into a large property named Goodlands situated in Bagatelle Road. The Carmel de Saint-Pair was founded on September 21st 1894 by Mère Marguerite Bouzeran and four other nuns originally from the Carmel of Coutances, and according to the comprehensive work by P. Picot focusing principally on the life of Pauline Reynolds, an English nun who became one of the Saint-Pair Carmelites before the move to Jersey,[1] their new monastery at Saint-Pair had hardly been completed when they were forced to leave. The persecution of religious orders had left the Carmelites in a tough position; as Pauline Reynolds underlined on August 20th 1901:

> We cannot stay in France without people one day exposing us and saying we split from Rome. The Government obviously wants to create a division and establish a "Gallican Church". [...] I know that we will be blamed for leaving: People will say we are fleeing the danger. Others would blame us for staying and say we are indirectly bowing to the Freemasons.[2]

The nuns, including Pauline Reynolds and the founder of the Order, all fled to Jersey. However, before moving the entire group to the Island, three of them including Pauline Reynolds and their Prioress, Mère Eliza, visited Jersey in order to locate a suitable property. They arrived by boat from Granville on September 2nd 1901, and we are told they were given a warm reception by the *Dames de Saint-André* "who welcomed us like true sisters" and by the Oblate Fathers who knew of their need to find "a calm and isolated retreat which would be easy to enclose": the Oblates showed them around Goodlands, a large sprawling farm estate with extensive grounds which they could rent from the owners with no problems.[3] They all moved to Jersey on September 23rd 1901, travelling from Granville by boat, and settled into Goodlands; after a few days of intensive work, they were able to fence up the outside of the grounds in order to ensure total seclusion from the outside world. Pauline Reynolds' notes tell us they were visited every day by the Jesuit Fathers from both Maison Saint-Louis and Notre-Dame-de Bon-Secours College, and these would hold Mass and see to the nuns' confessions and other needs.

The move from Saint-Pair in the Diocese of Coutances to Jersey, now under the Diocese of Portsmouth, also meant they had to build up new relations with their superiors, and according to the Archives of the Order, contact between the nuns and the Bishop's House in Portsmouth was upheld in a most positive manner. They were even visited by Mgr John Baptist Cahill, Bishop of Portsmouth, on one occasion. As far as their spiritual needs were concerned "Goodlands became our Eden"[4] and Pauline Reynolds acted as their interpreter for all things material and practical.

Sketch of Villa Ker Maria at Goodlands by Sr Isabelle from the Carmel of Saint-Pair, early 1900s (Courtesy of the Carmel of Saint-Pair)

Lodged mainly in the villa named Ker Maria at Goodlands, they wanted to build an extension to the property – they longed for a proper chapel of their own. However, as tenants and not owners, they were not permitted to make any major alterations to the house. Furthermore, the owners were constantly indicating that they wanted to sell Goodlands, and this left the nuns feeling insecure and unsure of what their future would hold. "This abnormal situation of being like birds on a branch lasted for four years"[5] until 1905 when Pauline Reynolds and Mère Eliza were able to collect enough funds to actually purchase the property. They then set about building a chapel on the grounds of Ker Maria, and it was officially blessed on May 24th 1906 by the Jesuit priest Père H. Troussard from Maison Saint-Louis (acting on behalf of the Bishop of Portsmouth), "accompanied by Père Rameau, Chaplain of the Carmel, and by several scholastics from Maison Saint-Louis."[6]

The correspondence between the Carmelites of Saint-Pair and the new Bishop of Portsmouth, William Timothy Cotter, indicates further positive interaction between the Order and the Diocese of Portsmouth, and a number of the letters from the Bishop go well beyond purely discussing formal issues, giving us an interesting insight into the personality of the Bishop as well as exterior events; in November 1918 for example, we learn of the devastating effects of the Spanish Flu epidemic in the Portsmouth region, and the fact that none of the Carmelites in Jersey were in any way affected by the deadly virus, most likely because they were protected from it by their secluded existence. Some of the Saint-Pair Carmelites did pass away during the nineteen years of exile, and these included the founder of the Order, Mère Bouzeran as well as Pauline Reynolds, Mère Thérèse de Jésus. Their tomb is in Almorah Cemetery.

Hautmont House, formerly a convent for Carmelites from St. Brieuc

The Carmel of Saint-Brieuc initially moved into a property in Bagatelle Lane called Ker Anna. It is understood that these nuns were the most affluent of the three groups who came; in 1907, reportedly finding the premises of Ker Anna unsuitable, they purchased a large house situated at Mont Millais called Hautmont.[7] The main building, constructed in the early 1860s, was comparatively modern and spacious, and was one of the finest houses in the area. A chapel, known as The Cloisters, was added by the Carmelites shortly after their arrival. The grounds also housed a cemetery.[8] An insight into the lifestyle of the nuns at Hautmont as well as the subsequent construction of the chapel can be found in George W. Croad's book, *A Jersey Album*:

> Suddenly the fine gates were closed, not to be opened for thirty five years. The railings were lined with corrugated iron, each sheet being serrated along its top edge, and the whole painted grey, while all climbable walls surrounding the property were also raised with similar sheeting. This privacy was required because the Carmelites were a closed order, with hardly any communication with the outside world. [...]
>
> Soon after their arrival the nuns began building on the North Gable. The builder was a local man of the same religious thinking as the Carmelites. His name was Mr. Peter Jouanne, of Five Oaks [...]
>
> The Carmelites being a closed order, elaborate precautions were in force to preserve their privacy, but workmen had to come in. The doors, or certain doors, could apparently only be unlocked from the inside; there was also an elaborate system for parcels, goods etc to be passed through hatches without even visible recognition between the messenger and the sisters; this even extended to movements of the "host".[9]

The Carmelites of Saint-Pair returned to France in 1920, those from Tours in 1933. The St. Brieuc Carmelites living at Hautmont remained in Jersey until after the German Occupation, and returned to France by fishing boat in two parties, on October 15th and November 4th 1945.

Bon Secours College

In October 1900, when Bon Secours Naval School based at Highlands was obliged to leave the Island, the premises were vacated and the building left empty. As a result of this, the Jesuits living at Maison Saint-Louis decided to use the building for the training of novices mainly from Laval. Novices from other scholasticates in France – in particular from Fourvière and the Lyons Province – came to the College too, and they stayed at the Bon Secours base until August-September 1906 when all the novices moved to new establishments.

In 1903, the Jesuits decided to make further use of the College premises: they decided to open a private boarding school for French boys of secondary-school age who were preparing for their official examinations. It was rightly believed by the Jesuits that such a project would appeal to the parents of boys in France who would not otherwise have been able to give their children the Jesuit education they desired for them because of the anticlerical laws in France. In the spring of 1903 the Jesuits sent a circular letter to parents along with a prospectus. The school opened in October that year with 23 pupils, the oldest of whom was twelve. Two years later, they had 73 pupils.

By 1906, the Jesuits were aware that the school building was beginning to become cramped, and this led to the departure of the novitiate. To gain extra space for the students and library they also managed to bypass a Jersey law of October 3rd 1901 which forbade foreign religious orders from erecting new permanent buildings: they simply put up buildings in corrugated iron which could easily be dismantled.

The school was exacting in both discipline and academic demands, and involved a strict religious routine; it also encouraged the development of sport amongst its students, an area which was often neglected at schools in France. Bon Secours College, as it was known, produced some outstanding students, its reputation grew in size and stature, and after 1914 when many Jesuit schools closed down in northern France, numbers increased radically. According to Eileen Nicolle, "between 1903 and 1919 as many as 1025 students had passed through the school."[10]

A tragic accident occurred on July 7th 1915. The college choirboys were given the afternoon free, a reward for all the efforts they had recently made at religious services; pupils and teachers went to spend a few hours on the beach at Portelet. Within minutes of the boys entering the sea, a huge swell swept away seven of them, and despite attempts by a teacher to rescue them, they all drowned. An eighth boy, one of the senior pupils, perished in an attempt to save the other seven. The death of eight boys all aged between ten and fifteen was a tragic blow for the College and for the Island as a whole. Amongst the dead boys were the sons of two local merchants.[11] This tragedy, occurring during such a vulnerable period of world history, heightened a feeling of solidarity between Islanders of all denominations. Heartache united

Islanders again in 1918 during the outbreak of Spanish Flu which cost the lives of many Jersey residents including two Bon Secours priests. The College's contribution to the 1914-1918 War effort in which 80 of the 350 mobilised by the French Government lost their lives, did not go unnoticed by the Jersey authorities. During the duration of World War I, the Lt Governor of Jersey showed his respect for the College and its role in Jersey life by paying a number of official and unofficial visits.

Memorial service for the eight Bon Secours pupils drowned in 1915
(Courtesy of Gerard Lecrivain)

World War I ended, and the College resumed a more normal life. But the effects of the War and recent tragedies had taken their toll on the school. On August 25th 1919, the Rector of the College, Père de Raucourt, sent a letter to all the pupils and their parents, informing them that the school would not re-open at the start of the new academic year. Financial difficulties caused mainly by an unfavourable exchange rate were the main cause. The College decided to move back to France. Post-war freedom in France had relaxed many of the anticlerical laws, and under the considerable financial strain they were suffering in Jersey, it seemed the only logical solution.

The priests and students from Bon Secours found themselves sent to various places of education in France. The students went to study at the college nearest their parents' home; some priests moved to Paris; the Rector, Père de Raucourt, went to Evreux, where the St. François de Sales College continued the work of Jersey's Bon Secours and even set up an Old Boys Association.

Teilhard de Chardin

One of the most prominent students of the novitiate at Bon Secours and the seminary at Maison Saint-Louis was Pierre Teilhard de Chardin. Born on May 1st 1881 at the family château in Sarcenat in the heart of the French Auvergne, he was educated at home before going to the Jesuit College of Notre Dame de Mongré at Villefranche-sur-Saône. On March 20th 1899 he entered the Jesuit novitiate in Aix-en-Provence in the Province of Lyons. First vows followed in 1901 during his juniorate period at Laval just as the major anti-clerical storm was about to break in France.

The Society of Jesus thought it prudent to withdraw its students from France and Teilhard and his *confrères* found themselves spending the next few years in Jersey – he started in his second-year at Bon Secours (1901-1902) and studied philosophy for a further three years at Maison Saint-Louis (1902-1905). It is also understood that his passion for geology was kindled whilst in Jersey. After receiving his degree, his *Licence-ès-lettres* from Caen University (to which many students from the Channel Islands went until the Second World War), Teilhard was sent to Egypt where he taught physics and chemistry at the Jesuit College of the Holy Family in Cairo (1905-1908) before returning to England in 1908. He spent the next four years studying theology at the Jesuit scholasticate at Ore Place, Hastings, which is where all the Bon Secours students originally from the Lyons Province were sent. On August 24th 1911 Teilhard was ordained priest at Ore Place. In 1912 he returned to Paris to begin research work at the Natural History Museum with the palaeontologist Marcellin Boule. In December 1914 Teilhard was mobilised as a stretcher-bearer on the Western Front. It was during these war years that he began to record all his thoughts on theology, science and philosophy both in a diary and in letters to his cousin, Marguerite Teilhard-Chambon, who later edited them into a book: *Genèse d'une pensée* (*Genesis of a Thought*). In 1916 he wrote his first essay: *La Vie Cosmique* (*Cosmic Life*). He took his Jesuit vows in Sainte-Foy-lès-Lyon, on May 26th 1918.

In August 1919, he returned to Jersey and stayed at Maison Saint-Louis again, this time in order to write a major work: *Puissance spirituelle de la Matière* (*The Spiritual Power of Matter*). He later became a Professor of Geology in 1920 at the Catholic Institute of Paris and travelled extensively in China working with scientific projects concerning the evolution of man. One of Teilhard's works, *Le Phénomène Humain* (*The Phenomenon of Man*), presented a sweeping account of the unfolding of the cosmos. He abandoned a literal interpretation of Book of Genesis in favour of a metaphorical interpretation. This displeased certain officials in the Catholic Curia, who thought that it undermined the doctrine of original sin developed by Saint Augustine. Teilhard also invented terms such as "Christ Omega" and "noosphere". His position was opposed by his church superiors, and his work was denied publication during his lifetime by the Roman Holy Office. He died in exile in New York on April 10th 1955: it was Easter Sunday. His funeral three days later was attended by less than a dozen people, but the literary, theological and philosophical legacy left by the former student of Jersey's Jesuit schools was enormous. As Siôn Cowell expresses in an article on the British Teilhard Association's website:

> Member of the Society of Jesus, Teilhard is probably one of the most written-about Jesuits of all time. And he is certainly one of the most controversial Jesuits of the twentieth century. After his death, his religious writings, once banned by his religious superiors, have sold in their millions and have been translated into every major language. His influence on the Second Vatican Council (1962-1965) is undoubted.[12]

Les Frères de l'Instruction Chrétienne de Ploërmel

The presence of the Brothers of Christian Instruction of Ploërmel (*Les Frères de l'Instruction Chrétienne de Ploërmel*) in Jersey had been welcomed and appreciated by the French Oblates in Jersey ever since their arrival in 1896 when they took over the running of a number of schools in the Catholic Parishes of the Island. Two Brothers and a lay teacher ran the Berry House School from 1896-1901 and again from 1903-1916. They had also actively assisted the teaching staff at Bon Secours College between 1906 and 1919 and worked at the Oblate Fathers' Secondary School at St. Mary's House, Roussel Street between 1910 and 1912. Additionally, they had helped to teach at St. Martin's Catholic School (1898-1900, 1901-1905) as well as at St. Matthew's (1897-1906). For seven years, some of the Brothers were employed at the Orphanage, some teaching gardening while others took charge of the dormitories and helped in the general running of the house. An article in the *Jersey Catholic Record* of May 1972 by Frère J.F. Libert makes reference to one of the Brothers' most eminent horticulture students in Jersey – Philip Le Troquer, later to become the Sacré Cœur Orphanage's Head Gardener.[13]

On February 12th 1904, a number of the Brothers fled France and arrived in Jersey, unsure of their next move as their mother-house in Ploërmel had just been shut down. Between March 12th and 15th, the Council of Brothers held a decisive meeting in Jersey, at premises they now occupied at 3, Victoria Street, a stone's throw from St. Thomas' Church.[14] This meeting was to establish a path for the future of the Brothers in the wake of the dramatic secularisation of French religious orders. Presided over by Frère Abel, the meeting's main concern was how to place the large numbers of Brothers who had recently fled the expulsions. Once in Jersey, they knew they could not return to France via St. Malo, and plans were drawn to move various groups to different locations; places they had in mind were missionary houses run by Jesuits in India and the Rocky Mountains, USA.

The Institute of Brothers of Christian Instruction of Ploërmel (also known as the De La Mennais Brothers or FIC), was founded by Jean-Marie Robert de Lamennais, a French Catholic priest, brother of the philosopher Felicité Robert de Lamennais. He was born in St. Malo on September 8th, 1780. From an early age he decided that he wanted to be a priest in spite of the hardship of the Revolution and the persecution that the clergy was suffering. His family gave refuge to priests in hiding. On February 25th, 1804, Jean-Marie de Lammenais was ordained a priest. His major concern was the education of poor Breton children, and schooling was to remain his main goal for the rest of his life. Together with another priest, Père Gabriel Deshayes, vicar of Auray, he founded the Brothers of Christian Instruction on June 6th 1819, their aim being to educate the youth of Brittany. He chose as motto for the new congregation, "Dieu Seul" – "For God Alone", often abbreviated to DS. In November 1824, thanks to an acquisition by Père Deshayes, Lammenais was able to open a motherhouse in Ploërmel, in the Morbihan region of Brittany. Over the years, the order widened its horizons, moving (often by necessity) beyond the confines of Brittany, and extended its missionary teaching work throughout the world. At the time of Lammenais' death on December 26th 1860, his congregation had over 800 members.

When the training college in France closed down in 1903, it was transferred to England, firstly to Taunton in Somerset, then in 1911 to St. Mary's College, Bitterne Park, Southampton.[15]

In 1919, when the Bon Secours Secondary School was closed, the buildings were put up for sale. The Superiors of the Brothers, now based at Ashton House, Rouge Bouillon, had already looked at other properties in the Island, but when they came and inspected the premises at Highlands, they deemed them ideal for both the training school and novitiate. In accordance with Jersey's financial legislation, a committee of five Brothers, all of whom were British subjects, purchased the property on June 9th 1922. The Superiors moved out of Ashton House and settled into the main building at Bon Secours – Cardwell House which was renamed St. Joseph's that same year.[16] *L'Echo des Missions des Frères de l'Instruction Chrétienne*, the Brothers' monthly publication, describes the departure from Southampton on the morning of August 17th 1922. Led by Frères Daniel and Roland, the students travelled to Jersey on the Caesarea, their goods and furniture having been packed up at St. Mary's College the night before. In spite of a rough crossing, they arrived in St. Helier at 9 am and reached the chapel at Notre-Dame-de-Bon-Secours after a 25-minute walk. The article tells us they spent that first afternoon exploring the Island and relaxing on the beach at Grève d'Azette, "searching the horizon in the hope of catching a glimpse of Dinard beach or the oyster beds at Cancale. But to see our dear France, one has to go to Bouley Bay or Mont Orgueil, and from there one can discern the Cotentin peninsula."[17]

The Jersey house became the international headquarters and study centre for students and teaching staff alike. The vast library of over 30,000 books was set up in one of the temporary out-buildings, and another of these *"zingos"*[18] was used as sleeping accommodation for visiting Brothers during spiritual retreats.[19] Most of the members were French, but over the years the Lammenais Brothers at Bon Secours schooled many young men from Italy, Haiti, the Seychelles, French Polynesia, Great Britain, the Americas and the Far East. When it opened in 1922 three were 117 students, very soon the numbers soared to 250.

A number of Brothers and other members of the Bon Secours entourage in Jersey died in the Island over the years, and when Frère Edbert died on January 24th 1924, a cemetery was inaugurated in the grounds. The Bon Secours Cemetery was blessed by Mgr Cotter of Portsmouth on June 20th 1931; the bodies of others, who had previously been buried at Almorah Cemetery, were transferred to the Bon Secours site on July 3rd 1933. These included the body of Frère Abel (Jean-Marie Gaudichon) who had died in 1910.

Until 1939 when World War II was declared, life for the Brothers of Christian Instruction of Ploërmel and their students at Bon Secours was highlighted by stability and increasing interaction with local Jersey residents. Part of Jersey life since 1896, they had, as Frère J.F. Libert points out in his article in the *Jersey Catholic Record,* moved from a position of "original mistrust" to one where they had "won the hearts of Jerseymen."[20]

The Observatory and Weather Tower

Père Marc Dechevrens, the scientist Jesuit priest and inventor who founded both the Observatory building and the Weather Tower, died on December 6th 1923. After his death, it appeared nobody was able to match his enthusiasm and stature. Furthermore, the Jesuits, who also had a major Observatory in China, maintained that it would be too costly to keep two observatories running with the same intensity. The Chinese Observatory at Zi-Ka-Wei was given priority, and some of the Jersey students were sent to China to continue work there. Over the next year, weather readings at St. Louis Observatory were considerably reduced. Then, in 1924, Père Christian Burdo arrived in Jersey.[21] A keen scientist and archaeologist who had previously studied in the Island at the Bon Secours novitiate, Père Burdo kept the Observatory running along with the assistance of the mathematics and physics master. Recordings started again on January 1ˢᵗ 1925, and Père Burdo remained Director for a total of eight years, although the number of recordings was reduced to three per day, compared to the eight per day in the Observatory's heyday under Père Dechevrens.

The Weather Tower, on the other hand, had suffered neglect during World War I. It badly needed costly repairs and repainting. As Père Charles Rey, the future champion of the Observatory, explained in an article published in *Jersey Church History*:

> In 1920 I undertook with some fellow students to hammer out rust and repaint the metal, beginning at the top, as no workmen could be found to undertake this somewhat perilous job. Later, when the working level was nearer the ground, plenty of labour was available, and it seemed that the tower still had a long spell of life. It was not to be.
>
> The expenses of keeping it in good condition of repair were too high, and it was decided that it should be pulled down. There was at some point a hope of reprieve. Only the top part, the most unsafe, would be taken down, leaving the structure two thirds of its original height.[22]

Within a few months, the *Jersey Morning News* reported this piece of news:

> If you wake up one morning and can't see what we call the Jesuits' Tower (for want of a better name) don't imagine your eyesight has gone wrong. This old landmark has apparently outlived its usefulness, due no doubt to wireless(!) – For I hear that the owners are seeking suitable offers to have the tower taken down as far as the second tier. Demolishing such a structure from the top is not an easy business short of pitching it over in sections and I doubt if the material saved would pay for the gear and labour needed to demolish it piecemeal.[23]

However, the plans to keep two-thirds of the Tower proved far too risky and expensive; the Jesuits at Maison Saint-Louis had tried to offer the Tower to the States of Jersey, but this was declined. Ultimately, on February 20ᵗʰ 1929, the Tower was completely dismantled by A.O.

Hill of the Dockyard, Dover. As the *Jersey Evening Post* reported:

> The Jesuits' Tower has gone, for at 11 o'clock this morning, one of the finest landmarks the Island possessed, swayed after a couple of seconds as the cables and tackle were tightened and then began to fall, finally to crash in the exact place which had been marked out for its fall. [...]
>
> So the Tower which was erected nearly 35 years ago is now nothing but a mass of twisted iron. The work of erecting it was carried out by a Belgian firm in 1894... the work of demolition occupied just 24 hours, but a great deal of breaking up requires to be done before the iron can be shipped to England. There is believed to be 40 odd tons.[24]

As for the Observatory, Père Burdo kept it running until 1933 when he retired as Director. In 1934, the directorship of the Observatory was taken over by Père Charles Rey.

Père Charles Rey

Père Charles Rey was born in Dakar, Senegal in 1897, the son of a French colonial official. He studied physics and philosophy at Maison Saint-Louis and also worked in the astronomical Observatory. After missionary work and further training in astronomy in Madagascar, he returned to Jersey in 1934 as Director of the Observatory and worked there for the next 47 years.[25] Meteorology was his speciality, but his experience in seismology in Madagascar led him

Père Charles Rey, 1897-1981
(Courtesy of Peter Abrams)

to introduce a seismograph to the Observatory; in June 1936 he made the first recordings of an earthquake near the Kamchatka Peninsular, some 5450 miles away. The seismograph used by Père Rey weighed more than a ton and was set deep into the rock in the basement of the Observatory. Originally lent to the Observatory by the Science Faculty of Strasbourg[26] for a period of two years, the seismograph is believed to still be in use here in Jersey.

De La Salle College – The Beeches

In 1896 the Brothers of Ploërmel had taken over the running of the boys' schools left vacant after the departure of the De La Salle Brothers. Between 1896 and 1917 when the De La Salle Brothers returned to Jersey, much had changed within the education laws in the Island: the States had taken control of all primary schools, and all tuition had to be in English with French as a subsidiary language. Furthermore, the teachers were required to have the English Teaching Certificate. This had forced the closure of many Catholic schools, and Berry House near St. Thomas' Church was now operated more or less single-handedly by one lady, Mme Durand. She only had ten pupils at the school. In 1917, Père Louis Gullient, who had already revived Catholic education in other sectors of the Island in previous years, was now Rector of St. Thomas' Parish; together with the help of Bro Charlemagne Léon, the Lasallian Director of Les Vauxbelets in Guernsey,[27] and the financial aid of Jerseyman Louis Jules Sangan,[28] who also used his position as British subject to open a new school, the French Brothers were given permission to reside and teach in Jersey as long as the staff had the required qualifications and would abide by the British education system. The assistant Brother Anthime Louis was given the responsibility of starting the new school – he had worked in America from 1907 to 1911, in Plymouth from 1911 to 1914, and he had been based in London between 1914 and 1917 organising study plans for French-language students needing to take English examinations. He had the necessary experience.

Once permission had been granted, they decided to search for a suitable property. This did not take long. Located a matter of yards from Beaulieu Convent to the south, and the Westbourne Terrace Carmelite Convent to the north, was a large house with extensive grounds. Once again, "Holy Hill" seemed the ideal location for a Catholic establishment. The house, The Beeches, belonged to an English lady residing in London, Mrs. K. Fellows. A Committee was set up known as the Board of Trustees, and The Beeches was acquired for the Brothers on September 1ˢᵗ 1917. However, Jersey laws required an interim period of three months before a property could be fully purchased. So in the meantime, Louis Sangan arranged for Berry House to be made available to the Brothers, and on September 29ᵗʰ 1917, three Brothers, Edward, Peter and Francis (from Dover) arrived in Jersey and moved into Berry House. The school was re-christened St. Aloysius College in honour of Père Louis Gullient. School started on October 1ˢᵗ 1917 with twelve pupils in two classes. It was decided that in spite of the school having a French background, all curriculum work would follow the British guidelines. By Christmas, there were 17 students, by Easter the school had 23, and at the start of the Summer Term, there were 37 pupils registered.

Berry House (Courtesy of St. Thomas' Church)

In the *Jersey Morning News* of September 12th 1918, the following announcement was made:

> The Beeches, situated in its own extensive and beautiful grounds, is absolutely ideal for the purpose of a School. The building is comparatively new and delightfully modern from the all-important point of hygenics. The classrooms are bright, roomy and well ventilated, while the dormitories have the same distinctive advantages. We wish the College and those at its head all possible success.[29]

The school in Plymouth where Frère Anthime Louis had worked between 1911 and 1914 had been shut down, so all the furniture was transported to Jersey and used at The Beeches. On September 16th, St. Aloysius College and The Beeches merged and opened with 57 pupils. Three more Brothers from Dover joined the staff. The College, like the rest of Jersey, was severely hit by the Spanish Flu epidemic of 1918, but there were no deaths. The first year proved to be successful, and by September 1920, there were 85 pupils registered. 1920 saw two important events mark the school year – firstly, the visit of Bishop Cotter of Portsmouth; secondly, the death of the College's founder, Frère Anthime Louis.

The College, which had no chapel of its own, initially sent pupils and teachers to services at the Carmelite Chapel at 4, Westbourne Terrace, a residence which later became the Brothers' house.[30] They then decided to attend chapel services at Beaulieu, where the *Auxiliatrices des Ames du Purgatoire* were based; this was deemed a more convenient arrangement for all concerned, considering the Carmelites were an enclosed order and needed privacy. In addition, it is noted in the school's records that the Carmelites were not altogether impressed with their neighbours and were wont to complain about footballs and cricket balls landing in their gardens.

Interaction between the College and the Parish of St. Thomas can be recorded throughout these early years both with regard to Church and leisure activities. A school chaplain was appointed from St. Thomas'. In 1921, the College produced its first annual play at the *Cercle St-Thomas*. And in spite of the need to adhere to a British curriculum, links with France were upheld at all times, and there is no doubt the bias was highly Francophile. The presence of the French Consul on Sports Day was a regular fixture.

In 1923, extensions were added to the College grounds - it was decided to close St. Aloysius College at Berry House and unite the two schools at The Beeches. By now, the College had a combined number of 164 pupils. On November 24th 1924 the new buildings were completed, and on December 23rd the boys from St. Aloysius moved into their new classrooms. The final fusion of The Beeches and St. Aloysius took place in 1929 when the whole college was officially named De La Salle College.

The Thirties saw more development. In 1934 the Assembly Hall was built. The school now had 221 pupils. By 1938, the College was able to celebrate its 21st birthday, and could congratulate itself on having achieved growth and success, maintaining a balance between British education, French background and Catholic pastoral care.

De La Salle College (The Beeches)

7 Departures, Arrivals and Struggles

New Laws in Jersey

1911 was another year of major upheaval in Jersey's Catholic community, one which upturned much of the stability which had been built up since the turn of the century despite various attempts by the States of Jersey to place restrictions on the Catholic schools.[1] New laws were passed in the States which clearly stated that all education in the Island had to be administered in English, and that members of staff had to be both fluent in English and have the English Teaching Certificate. Furthermore, the States stipulated that "no grant would be paid except to those schools which the States were then building, and on the condition that no dogma, prayer or ceremony of any religious denomination be taught or tolerated."[2] Additionally, fines could be (and were) imposed on those parents who sent their children to Catholic schools which did not meet these guidelines. Numbers were dwindling at the Catholic schools, and after much deliberation, Bishop Cotter of Portsmouth decided that the French-speaking *Dames de Saint-André* would have to leave Jersey and be replaced by English-speaking teachers. He contacted a group of Faithful Companions of Jesus who had been living in Guernsey since 1907. These Sisters had fled their motherhouse at Ste Anne d'Auray in Brittany as a result of the anti-clerical laws, and had established a school at Les Touillets, Guernsey.

The FCJ Sisters move to Jersey

The Society of Sisters Faithful Companions of Jesus was founded in Amiens in France in 1820 by Marie Madeleine de Bonnault d'Houet,[3] a nun who wished to bring into being a Society that would take the name of Jesus and follow the constitutions of the Jesuits. Her decision to do this aroused great opposition, but despite all her difficulties, the Society of the Sisters Faithful Companions of Jesus was created, and Marie Madeleine began her work in Amiens with two companions, a school teacher, and seven children who received religious education; these were taught to read, write and sew, and were trained in domestic service. The Society flourished and grew in stature.

In 1830, ten years after the first beginnings of the Society, France was in religious turmoil again, and Marie Madeleine feared for the safety of her community. She was advised to establish a base in another country and so the Society began to spread, first to England, then to Italy, Switzerland and Ireland. In all, during her lifetime, twenty seven convents were established by the founder herself. It was as a result of the bases in England and Ireland that the FCJ Sisters developed strong bonds with the English-speaking world, and many of the Sisters living at the motherhouse in Sainte Anne d'Auray at the time of the evacuation in 1907 were of English or Irish origin, and almost all were totally bilingual.

When Bishop Cotter invited the FCJ Sisters to move from Guernsey to Jersey, he warned their Superior General, Mère Zoë Girod, that if she accepted his invitation "it would be an act of heroism."[4] All the schools would need teachers, and these not only included the town schools but those in the countryside: St. Matthew, St. Ouen, Hautes Croix, St. Aubin, St. Martin and Grouville. The majority of the school buildings were by now the property of the *Dames de Saint-André* who sold everything directly to the FCJ Sisters. The thirty-two *Dames de Saint-André* who had been living in Jersey left the Island, some moving to England where they had houses, others later moved to Brazil where a new teaching institution was founded before the outbreak of World War I. The FCJ Sisters arrived in Jersey on July 29th 1911 and settled into the premises sold to them by the *Dames de Saint-André*, and by May 1912 the number of pupils at the schools had almost doubled. That same month, the boarding school, still described in the Annals of the FCJ Sisters as "the little colony of Ste Anne",[5] was set up in a large property, La Bagatelle, overlooking St. Clement's Bay.[6] The premises at Bagatelle housed the main "headquarters" for the FCJ community, and were home to a boarding school principally for French girls, working in tandem with the Jesuit Bon Secours College for boys. The sister of Charles Rey (the Jesuit priest who later achieved fame in

Bagatelle Convent FCJ / Palace Hotel (Private Collection)

Students at Bagatelle Convent FCJ (Private Collection)

the field of meteorology at the Observatory) was a pupil at the school whilst her two brothers were educated at Bon Secours. The school at Bagatelle was known for its impressive gardens, enlarged by the first Chaplain who created rustic bridges over the stream and made seats under the trees. All the furniture which had been brought from Ste Anne d'Auray to Guernsey was then re-housed at Bagatelle, and a large statue of St. Philomena sent from the Society's cradle in Amiens, was placed on one of the gables. A new wing was added to the eastern side of the building, large enough to fit another fifteen or so rooms. This building work was carried out by Peter Jouanne of Five Oaks, the same man who had undertaken the work for the Carmelites at Hautmont. The Superior of the FCJ Sisters was the larger-than-life Mother Magdalen Harding, "a powerful woman, physically and mentally. She went round driving her little cart and pony!"[7] – often described in colourful terms by those who recalled her presence in the Island. George Croad, in his *Jersey Album*, mentions the fact that she was nicknamed "The Dreadnought" by many Islanders who would see her sweeping into the market to sell vegetables from the grounds at Bagatelle.

Besides teaching in the elementary schools, the Sisters also started Sunday schools. On Easter Sunday 1914 they began classes at St. Martin's, and in the same year, two Sisters started to go to St. Aubin's for Catechism classes. Two years later, in May 1916, a similar initiative was begun at Grouville. There were three main FCJ establishments in Jersey: Bagatelle, St. Matthew and Val Plaisant, giving scope for interchange and hospitality amongst staff and pupils. For example, those pupils from Bagatelle who stayed in Jersey for the holidays, frequently spent some time at St. Matthew's.

At the same time as the boarding school at Bagatelle was starting to receive French pupils, the large convent at Val Plaisant / David Place was beginning its career as an English establishment. Initially there were two secondary schools – a boarding school and a day school, but in 1919 they were amalgamated, and from that time onwards, numbers increased rapidly. A newspaper advertisement for the school stressed the school would be preparing its students for a wide range of academic examinations including the London Matriculation and Oxford Locals, the Royal College of Music and the Royal Drawing School. Additionally, "attention is given to physical development; Net-Ball, Hockey and Tennis are encouraged." The advertisement also added that "the School has for its aim to combine Catholic influence and character training with the surroundings of a refined home and up-to-date-education."[8]

The first few years at St. Matthew's were marked by excellent rapports between the Oblates and the FCJ Sisters. The school was promising. A copy of its prospectus (in English) found in the Archives of the Diocese of Portsmouth advertised the fact that it was "situated on an eminence in a most healthy part of the Island and is within convenient distance of St. Helier. The French language receives particular attention. English is taught in all its branches."[9] Many parents of both Jersey and French background sent their girls there, and by October 1915 the success led to the amalgamation of the boys' and girls' schools at St. Matthew's.

St. Matthew's Church and Convent, 1923 (Courtesy of Mike Edmunds)

Internal Tension

Over the course of the years, it appears from various documentary sources that rifts began to develop between the French Oblates based at St. Matthew's and the FCJ Sisters at the Convent. Despite the fact that they only lived across the road from each other and had frequent contact as a result of the Oblate Chaplain holding Mass for the Sisters at the Convent chapel, communication was often tense. Petty squabbles between them occurred frequently. One such dispute was over furniture apparently borrowed by the Sisters and not returned to the Oblates at the presbytery, and is reported at length by the Oblates in the unpublished *Codex Historicus*. It was obvious that for a number of reasons, the Oblates sorely missed the *Dames de Saint-André*. Additional problems were brought about by bureaucratic, financial and legal difficulties which were largely caused by catalytic decisions taken by the States of Jersey. These problems did not contribute to mend relations between the Oblates and the FCJ Sisters which were already becoming quite strained. However, these disagreements were seemingly trivial compared to the events which occurred between 1919 and 1923.

On December 23rd 1919, the States of Jersey announced that all country Catholic primary schools in Jersey would close that day and not be re-opened. This announcement obviously came as a shock to all concerned, and is reported in detail in the *Codex*:

> Today is the worst day St. Matthew's Mission has known since it was founded. At five minutes past twelve noon, Balleine, the Secretary of the Education Committee for Primary Education, arrived at the Convent of the Faithful Companions and asked to speak to Mother Berchmans; he told her: "At 4pm today the school will close and will never re-open." The same decision was taken for the school at St. John, Hautes-Croix.
>
> It is persecution! It will disperse our children in Protestant schools [...] It will be difficult, almost impossible to give our children a Catholic education. The law permits the Priest to teach catechism classes in the schools, but the abominable law requires this to take place between 9.15 and 9.45 am.[10]

Aware of the fact that there were ten Protestant elementary schools within St. Matthew's Parish alone, the Oblates knew that this task would be a huge challenge. They did not accept the new law without making an appeal. A petition sent to the Lieutenant Governor, Major General A. Wilson, the Bailiff, William V. Vernon, and the States of Jersey was lodged *au Greffe* on February 17th 1920. Signed by Canon John Hourigan on behalf of Bishop Cotter, it protested vehemently at the closure of the schools. The petition had no effect. So the task in hand had to be met: a *Codex* entry of February 1921 describes how the work was divided amongst the various Oblates. Père Pierre Guéret who was based at Hautes-Croix would work at two schools between the stipulated times, Père Félix Blaise Morard (in charge of St. Ouen's District), took on two schools, and Père Joseph Emile Pitard at St. Matthew's visited a total of five schools on a regular basis. This enabled approximately 220 children to receive Catholic education within the Parish, but it was obvious to the priests that the pupils were lacking the motivation they would have had were the system not so complicated. Fewer worshippers were attending Mass. The priests were becoming disheartened, both with the cause of the problem (the laws) and the lack of help they were receiving from other sources.

This was just the tip of the iceberg. The Oblates felt they should have had more assistance from the FCJ Sisters, and did not feel they were being offered enough solidarity:

> Are we being assisted elsewhere in our work of evangelising? Not one bit. In the old days, the Faithful Companions of Jesus living in the Convent near St. Matthew's Church, would teach the children – boys as well as girls – from our schools (St. Matthew, Hautes-Croix and St. Ouen), just as the dearly missed *Dames de Saint-André* before them. Since the closure of the schools, the Faithful Companions are only bothered with their boarding school which houses a few English and French girls – both Catholic and Protestant. The only other thing they do is supervise the children of St. Matthew's during services. They no longer turn up at our annexes at Hautes-Croix and St. Ouen.[11]

The diary entry continues for over two pages, lamenting the loss of the *Dames de Saint-André* and the apparent lack of *engagement* by the FCJ Sisters. The author of the diary, understood to be Père Pitard, also indicates that the FCJ Sisters, no longer wishing to take on the responsibility of the chapel-schools in St. Ouen and at Hautes-Croix, were contemplating a probable sale of these properties.

> What will become of our annexes at Hautes-Croix and St. Ouen? The Faithful Companions want to get rid of these closed schools which also happen to be our chapels. They wanted to sell them several months ago, but the price was preposterously high. The Bishop [Cotter] does not want to buy, nor do the Oblates.

The logical thing to do is rent out the buildings, as long as the owners, the Faithful Companions, charge a reasonable rent.[12]

The Oblates also complained of the lack of repair work on the buildings, noting that the Hautes-Croix property was in a precarious state and that nothing had been done to improve either the roof or the unstable door since the news of the schools' closures had been announced.

The third annexe which gave cause for concern was the chapel-school at St. Aubin. Until 1919 it had been part of the Parish of St. Thomas; however, when Père Alain Mao became Rector of St. Matthew's that same year, he asked for St. Aubin to be re-annexed to St. Matthew's Parish. Père Mao had a special fondness for St. Aubin, and since 1911 had longed to enlarge the church facilities in the area. Although the existing Sacré Cœur Chapel on Mont Les Vaux was satisfactory, his hope was to build a new church in the district bearing the same name. In fact, by 1912 he had already been in contact with a Parisian architect, Julien Barbier, renowned for his Neo-Gothic designs in various parts of France.[13] Barbier drew up plans for a new church that same year, and the original designs are in the Archives of St. Thomas' Church.

Between 1913 and 1919, the FCJ Sisters had run the school at St. Aubin. However, not all their decisions in the district were met with a positive response. They decided to work alongside the local Protestant school in St. Aubin, and in 1915, because of the illness and death of the headmaster of the Protestant school, they amalgamated the two establishments for secular subjects and for the duration of World War I. Travelling by train from the town, the Sisters would "reach the school each morning after a 20-minute drive round the lovely bay",[14] and would teach at both schools. Initially, this avant-garde arrangement did not please some of the more traditionalist and strict Catholics, such as the older generation of Oblates, who were quite horrified at this pact. The reactions were identical in the Protestant camp, and a number of complaints from the Protestant clergy were made. They found it disturbing that a Roman Catholic nun, Mère Xavier Collopy, should be running a Protestant school. Nevertheless, the decision to work together as a team has been regarded in some circles as a highly forward-thinking initiative, effectively marking the beginnings of a less sectarian approach to Christian fellowship.

In 1920 Père Joseph Emile Pitard became Rector of St. Matthew's, a post he would hold for thirteen years, and Père Mao became Superior at St. Thomas'; when he asked that St. Aubin's be re-instated as a part of St. Thomas' Parish, Bishop Cotter of Portsmouth refused, stating that it was impractical to move chapels from Parish to Parish on such a regular basis.[15] However, he did permit Père Mao to send a priest from St. Thomas' to serve St. Aubin's, as long as the chapel now remained firmly part of St. Matthew's. This seemed satisfactory to all concerned, and Père Brousquet of St. Thomas' was put in charge of St. Aubin's, travelling there by train from St. Helier. However, the extra chapel-school now in the Parish of St. Matthew's actually meant that this Parish had four empty schools under their wing as opposed to three, all of which belonged to the FCJ Sisters.

Sale of Schools

Tension between the Oblates of St. Matthew's and the FCJ Sisters mounted. The Sisters argued they could not afford the upkeep of all these country properties which were not being used. The Oblates felt they were being betrayed by the Sisters who were prepared to sell off chapels and schools to total strangers (and possibly Protestant ones!) rather than reach some compromise with the Church. The feud became bitter. On February 14th 1922, a letter from the Oblate Provincial to Père Pitard underlined the fact that they did not have the funds to cover the purchase of the two chapels under discussion – St. Ouen and Hautes-Croix. On July 23rd that year, the annual pilgrimage to St. Anne's Chapel in St. Ouen was held as normal amidst mixed feelings. A newspaper advertisement had just informed the Island's readers that four buildings – St. Ouen, St. John, St. Aubin and St. Martin – were to go on sale. After a fraught summer, the four schools were put on the market on Friday, September 22nd 1922 by F. Le Gallais and Sons. The announcement in the press indicated that all four buildings could be ideally suited to domestic conversion. The sales went ahead.

The new owner of the former school at Hautes-Croix – a Protestant – allowed the Oblates to continue using the part of the building which had been their chapel for the period of a year, albeit at a rent of £25. They accepted, although the situation was far from satisfactory. A paper-thin wall separated the "chapel" from the living quarters of an elderly couple, who apparently would talk so loud in their dwelling that every word could be heard during Mass next door. In St. Ouen, an agreement was similarly arranged with the new proprietor, George Farrell, whereby they could temporarily rent a room in the building for £12 per annum. The chapel in St. Aubin was purchased in the name of Mgr Cotter by Père Mao, who could not bear the thought of his beloved St. Aubin losing its place of worship. In St. Martin, the old school building was successfully taken over by the Jesuit Fathers of Maison Saint-Louis who assisted Père Abel Pierrat, Rector of St. Martin, in setting up a Club and Patronage; a similar arrangement was met at St. Joseph's, Grouville.[16]

Ville à L'Evêque

The Oblates soon realised that they needed a new chapel to replace the one they had lost at Hautes-Croix, and in spite of severe financial difficulties largely caused by the unfavourable exchange rate, they were able to acquire a plot of land at Ville à L'Evêque in Trinity on November 11th 1922. This transaction was made in the name of Théophile Derrien who had the necessary qualifications to purchase Jersey land and who was also a generous benefactor. He was also one of the Parish organists, and his contribution to local Catholic life, and specifically the former chapel at Hautes-Croix, is often referred to in the *Codex*.[17] It is understood the foundation stone was laid in May 1923, the aim being to have a chapel in place by September 1923. The work was undertaken by a local Trinity man, a Mr. Cabot, and much of the granite used for the construction was quarried at Ronez. The building work was completed by the end of the year, and on January 6th 1924, it was officially blessed by Père Legrand; the first High Mass at Ville à L'Evêque was celebrated by Père Pitard of St. Matthew's. Père Guéret was given responsibility for the district.

Old photographs of the granite chapel show various developments between 1924 and 1926. At its official blessing in January 1924, the chapel did not have a bell tower; this was added in the latter half of 1926, the work having commenced in August. The bell itself was a gift from a teacher from Jarrow-on-Tyne (Durham), a Miss Marie Joseph Sydney MacFeely who had also donated a baptismal font for the new

Ville à L'Evêque Church in 1924 (Courtesy of St. Thomas' Church)

Construction of Bell Tower at Ville à L'Evêque Church in 1926 (Courtesy of Mike Edmunds)

Original sketch by Joseph Benoit for stained glass window at Ville à L'Evêque, 1927 (Courtesy of Mike Edmunds)

148

church in November 1925. The *Codex* informs us that the bell, weighing 50kg, was installed by Mr Jouanne of Five Oaks, and was named Marie-Thérèse; it was decorated with images of the Virgin Mary, St. Therese of the Child Jesus, St. John the Baptist and St. Anthony of Padua (the last two saints being the patrons of the former chapel at Hautes-Croix and the new one at Ville à L'Evêque). It was officially blessed by Mgr Alfred-Jean Guyomard, Bishop of Jaffna, on December 26th 1926, and its godparents were Miss MacFeely and Père Pitard. Various benefactors donated numerous artefacts to the chapel – these included a statue of St Thérèse of the Child Jesus created by the famed French sculptor Charles Desvergnes[18] (a gift from Théophile Derrien in May 1925), and two small altars in October that year. The *Codex Historicus* also informs us that further donations enabled them to purchase candlesticks and candelabras for the small altars in January 1926, as well as carpets for the nave.

During the springtime of 1927, three stained-glass windows were installed in the chapel. Largely funded through parishioners' generosity, the windows were blessed by Père J.A. Laillé shortly before Corpus Christi in 1927. These were the work of Joseph Benoit of Nancy, who was also commissioned around this time to produce the windows at St. Matthew's Church as well as another three windows for Ville à L'Evêque which were installed in October 1928. The first three windows depicted Notre-Dame-de-Sion, St. John the Baptist and St. Anthony, the second three depicted St. Joseph, St Thérèse of the Child Jesus and Jean-Baptiste-Marie Vianney (better known as the Curé d'Ars, or Vicar of Ars). Priests during this period included Père Laillé's successors, Père Cotarmanac'h, Père Constant Labbé and Père Joseph Mainville.

St. Ouen – A Wooden Chapel

With regards to St. Ouen, the Oblates felt they could no longer continue renting a small room in the former chapel-school, so they decided to set up a more permanent chapel; by 1924 they were able to fund a small wooden chapel in the same field as their former chapel-school. The material for this chapel came from France. The owner of the field, George Farrell, gave them permission to do so. The wooden chapel was officially opened on June 20th 1924. Mass was sung by Père Pitard,

Wooden Chapel – formerly St. Anne's Church, St. Ouen.
Later moved to Ville à L'Evêque (Private Collection)

Interior of the Wooden Chapel at St. Ouen, late 1920s
(Courtesy of Mike Edmunds)

Rector of St. Matthew's who also installed the Stations of the Cross with Mgr Cotter's permission. The Sacrament was blessed by Père Félix Morard who was in charge of St. Ouen. One month later, on July 20th 1924, St. Anne's Chapel was officially blessed by Père Mao. Over the course of the next few years numerous donations and gifts were made in aid of the chapel, the annual pilgrimage was upheld each year in honour of St. Anne, and Père Morard's successor, Père Yves Jaïn, who took over in 1926, took it upon himself to inject the district with added dynamism.

The "White Elephant" – St. Matthew's Convent

With working solutions now established in the local districts, it might have been assumed the Oblates were feeling more content with the state of affairs. This was not the case. At the backs of their minds loomed a major crisis which was soon to escalate rapidly. In May 1923, Mère Philomena, the Superior of the FCJ Sisters based at St. Matthew's Convent, informed Père Pitard that they would be closing the Convent during the course of the next few months. As Père Pitard wrote in the *Codex*:

> It is a disaster for the Parish which still possessed a small private school (25 young girls). [...] The house will probably be sold. To whom? I am afraid we may find ourselves with a Protestant school next door.[19]

On July 16th 1923 the boarding house and private school closed down. The Oblate Fathers were furious. In a lengthy and irate diary entry Père Pitard vented all his anger:

> Today saw the closure of the boarding house and private school run by the Faithful Companions of Jesus. Their explanation is that they can no longer afford it. But did they really need 12 nuns in a house containing 15 boarders and 25 day pupils? The real reason which they are not telling us is that they are founding a magnificent boarding school in England, and because of this, some secondary houses are being sacrificed. St. Matthew's has become a victim at a moment when the number of pupils

attending the day school was on the rise. [...] From now on we won't have a single Catholic school in the Parish. The States of Jersey have closed down St. John's, St. Ouen, St. Aubin and St. Matthew; the FCJs are finishing off the odious job by closing their boarding school and their private school: *Ad majorem Dei gloriam!* That is the motto of their Society.[20]

Shortly after this announcement was made, Père Mao at St. Thomas' decided to find out if he could locate a religious congregation in France (holding the necessary linguistic requirements) who could take over the Convent. He also sent a letter to Mère Philomena begging her to think twice before selling the Convent. The Superior's response was that they had tried, albeit unsuccessfully, to find a suitable Congregation based in England, but that none had been willing to purchase the Convent. Père Pitard felt that the main reason why nobody wanted to buy the Convent was the high price the Sisters were demanding – £6000. The Oblates did not have the financial backing to afford it, neither did any of the Congregations who were contacted.[21]

Over the next two months the FCJ Sisters, who maintained they did not have the means to support themselves at St. Matthew's, moved many of their belongings out of the premises. The school's furniture was sent to Bagatelle, other items of furniture were sold. A dealer in second-hand goods was called in to take away other pieces to sell at the market in St. Helier. Some goods were even bought by the Methodists. The only belongings left in the property were the religious statues and furnishings from the Convent chapel, although some of these were also moved out or sold. Two statues of St. Joseph and the Virgin Mary were sold to the De La Salle Brothers.[22] There was also an attempt at moving out the altar and exchanging it with a less ornate one from Bagatelle, although this was stopped by an exceedingly angry Père Pitard.

> I refused to let them treat Our Saviour in the same way as they had treated the Holy Virgin and St. Joseph, and only after I threatened to stop the Chaplain from visiting them if the altar left the house, did they agree to leave it be.[23]

By the end of the summer, the only functions taking place within the Convent were the religious services, still held regularly by the Sisters' Oblate Chaplain.

Reactions to the sales were mixed – the Sisters remained adamant that this was the only viable solution for them financially, were they to continue operating schools at Bagatelle and David Place; the Oblates became increasingly angrier and more vociferous as they witnessed the comings and goings of salesmen at the Convent directly opposite the presbytery.

Bishop Cotter with choirboys and French priests including Père Théodule Maré, Père Eugène Méline, Père Alain Mao, Père Jean-Louis Messager, Père Pierre Guéret and Père Yves Jaïn (Courtesy of St. Thomas' Church)

Until now, Mgr Cotter of Portsmouth had not commented on the situation; however, on September 14th 1923 he visited Jersey, and Père Pitard asked for assistance. The Bishop made it clear that he could not intervene, as the property did belong to the Sisters and they were free to sell it if they so wished. But he did offer to contact the Franciscan Missionaries of Mary who had many Canadian subjects as members; they might be interested in purchasing.

On September 25th, the Sisters halved their asking price, aware that nobody was making any offers. That same day, a member of the *Comité de l'Instruction Publique* arrived at the Convent by car. Within days, it was understood that the States of Jersey had decided to purchase the Convent and turn it into the new Home for Boys, a Protestant orphanage which sorely needed better accommodation. This was the last straw for the Oblates. They wrote to Bishop Cotter in Portsmouth. His reply, sent on September 27th 1923, read as follows: "You have intrigued me in the final destination of the "White Elephant." It is not my property, but I should set fire to it before giving it as you surmise."[24]

Within a few days, the sale of the property was announced publicly. All the Island's newspapers reported it. A lengthy article in the *Jersey Evening Post* concludes as follows:

> For those who did not know the place, he [the Committee President] could say it was an ideal place for a Home. The property was in good condition; it was a solid structure, which was built some years ago out of funds provided by benefactors of a certain religious belief. The price asked for the place was particularly cheap, and he felt they should feel proud of their bargain.[25]

Around the same date the *Chroniques de Jersey* referred to the sale as "une sage decision", and the Protestant *Jersey Critic* published an article loaded with irony aimed undoubtedly at the very public feud taking place between the Oblates and the FCJ Sisters:

The Home for Boys - A Good Stroke of Business:
The purchase of St. Matthew's Convent by the States is a good stroke of business.

The boys should be very well there - far better than where they are now. The building is modern and in most respects is well equipped. We understand that there are no bathrooms, and we had been told that the water supply was inadequate. Bathrooms, however, can be built (though not on the lines of the cement tank at the present Home, we trust), and Jurat Crill assured the States on Saturday that there was an excellent water supply.

It has been whispered to us, by the way, that many members of the Roman Catholic community in our midst are exceedingly angry. They wouldn't have minded the transfer of the place to an association of their own faith, but to see it pass into Protestant hands annoys them very much indeed.

And, when you come to think of it, it is very seldom that such a thing occurs; it is generally the other way round in Jersey.[26]

The Oblates became even more frustrated by the newspaper reports, and melodramatic diary entries in the *Codex* underline their anger which was directed at the FCJ Sisters and the consequences of their actions:

Our enemies are victorious. The above articles clearly show that. Is it not true that the sale of this house mirrors the crime of Judas as related in the Gospels? Judas too was the Faithful Companion of Jesus, he had the same title as the Faithful Companions of Jesus. This Congregation has acted like Judas throughout the whole of this affair, behaving slyly vis-à-vis the Oblates.[27]

The author of these *Codex* notes, Père Pitard, continued his frenzied outburst over a number of pages, using Biblical imagery whenever referring to the current situation. He likened the price received for the Convent (£3000) to the thirty pieces of silver given to Judas. One can only imagine the atmosphere at the final Mass held at the Convent, on Monday October 1st. It was Père Pitard himself who decided to take this final Mass rather than send the Chaplain, Père Guéret. Only five Sisters were present at the Mass, Mère Philomena herself being absent. Père Pitard's sermon basically accused the FCJ Sisters of having committed a grave wrongdoing by selling the Convent to Protestants, and he used the theme of Reparation to transmit his message.

In the meantime, Père Mao lodged an official appeal to the sale, and managed to postpone the signing of the deeds from October 5th to November 9th. On October 5th, the last of the Sisters left the Convent without bidding farewell to the Oblates across the road. The Convent was now completely empty.

Père Mao pursued his appeal and decided to send a letter to Rome in order to try and cancel the sale. It is understood that when Père Mao's letter reached the Cardinals and was forwarded to the Pope himself, the latter is said to have strictly opposed the sale of the Convent to a Protestant organisation, stressing the fact that the original purpose of the building as designed by those who constructed it, was purely and simply for Catholic education. This should be respected.

It appears that the appeals to Rome were successful; within a few days, the newspapers were sporting new advertisements informing readers that St. Matthew's Convent was to be put up for sale by Public Auction at the office of G.F.D. Le Gallais, 6 Hill Street, St. Helier, on Thursday, November 8th 1923. This news came as a shock to everyone concerned. Wasn't the Convent already sold? An explanation soon appeared in the press. On November 7th, *Les Chroniques de Jersey* concluded that the contract with the States had had to be broken because the owners had not obtained the necessary authorisation from Rome. The role of the building, built by a Catholic order with specific functions in mind, was to remain as such unless special authorisation had been granted by Rome itself. This also meant that *another* announcement appeared in the press, this time cancelling the latest sale advertisement which had suggested that the Convent could ideally be transformed into a first class hotel or sanatorium!

The Oblates calmed down, relieved that the Convent had been spared such a fearful fate, and the Convent remained empty and unsold for almost one year.

Les Soeurs de l'Immaculée Conception de Saint-Méen-Le-Grand

On October 25th 1924 the Convent was finally sold. After much negotiation, Mgr Cotter acquired the property for the sum of £3200 on behalf of a religious order: *L'Immaculée Conception de Saint-Méen-Le-Grand* – the Immaculate Conception of Saint-Méen-Le-Grand.

> At last, thanks to God and the intercession of the Blessed Thérèse of the Child Jesus who had been invoked quite specially for the circumstance, thanks too to the prayers said in particular by the former owners of the property, the *Dames de Saint-André*, the Convent is in good hands.[28]

The Congregation, attached to the Diocese of Rennes, was founded in 1831 by Pélagie Hélène Le Breton de Maisonneuve who was born in Quintin in 1789.[29] Under her religious name of Mère Saint-Félix, she founded the Congregation of the Immaculate Conception in the historic Breton town of Saint-Méen-Le-Grand, with its aims being to promote the education of young girls of every milieu, as well as participate actively and fully in many other areas of social life – these included nursing and family welfare.

On Monday October 27th 1924 at 8 o'clock in the morning, three Sisters of the Immaculate Conception arrived at the Convent. They had already been in Jersey for several days, and had stayed with the Brothers of Christian Instruction of Ploërmel at Bon Secours. Accompanied by Père Pitard, they entered their new abode, this being the first time Père Pitard had set foot inside the building since he held the final Mass there for the FCJ Sisters on October 1st 1923. The house, gardens and outside areas were all blessed that same day. The Sisters were given their official welcome into the Parish at High Mass on November 2nd. Limited to a maximum of six Sisters by a new Jersey law which would not allow more than that number to work in any given Parish, the Congregation settled into the Convent with a group of approximately 30 students – all girls – who were preparing their examinations in order to become active teaching nuns. The place effectively became a juniorate, and because the girls were all aged over 14, there were no Jersey laws to oppose their plans. Additionally, much to the delight of the Oblates, the Saint-Méen Sisters took on various Parish commitments including the supervision of the Children of Mary and teaching catechism classes on Saturdays and Sundays within the Parish.

On December 15th, Père Pitard blessed the Convent's chapel and held Mass there for the first time since October 1st 1923. This ceremony was attended by four Sisters and four pupils, and on December 26th, with Mgr Cotter's permission, the Stations of the Cross were installed in their chapel.

The Sisters and their students only stayed for one year, after which the students returned to France. Around four Sisters remained at the Convent and continued assisting the Oblates with catechism classes and the promotion of the various patronages and societies for young people. They were not permitted to open any new school of their own, and the Oblates felt that the States of Jersey were being hostile towards them in particular because of the events surrounding the aborted sale of the Convent in 1923. Living off the small amounts of money sent to them by the motherhouse in Saint-Méen, and earning very little in Jersey (mainly doing needlework and selling vegetables etc), the nuns were nevertheless eager to please the Oblates, and were held in high esteem by them. One *Codex* entry in the early months of 1927 indicates how they often reminded the Oblates of the *Dames de Saint-André*. The Sisters also helped the Jesuits at Maison Saint-Louis.

This continued for over ten years until 1937 by which time the Sisters, in particular Sr Agnès, were also helping out local pupils by giving them extra lessons. At about the same time, a Jersey lady, Mme Olympe Rose du Feu (whose ailing 14-year-old son Edward Francis was educated by her at home), decided to help other children who needed home tuition. Lacking space for this at her Mont Félard home, she sought help from the priests at St. Matthew's. They suggested using a room at the Convent, and by 1938, the two groups of pupils were united as a small school under one roof. The authorities allowed them to develop the project, and by the outbreak of World War II in 1939 Sr Agnès and Mme du Feu had the beginnings of a thriving private Catholic school. This venture was to become the beginning of a much larger scheme.

St. Matthew's Church

The church itself saw a number of developments during these years. In April 1909 Père Messager inaugurated the St. Matthew's Brigade and supervised its development over the years along with Colonel Pollock-Gore. Later, many of the members of the Brigade lost their lives on the Western Front. In 1912, in order to celebrate the 25th anniversary of Père Constant Le Vacon's arrival in Jersey, the parishioners of St. Matthew's collected enough funds to cover the cost of a new altar for the church. This new altar was designed by Pierre Rouillard of Angers and was sent over in sections for on-site assembly. In spite of an accident en route in which part of the altar was smashed and had to be re-designed in Angers, the work was completed during the summer of that year. It was consecrated by Bishop Cotter. During the 1920s a new cemetery was built adjoining the older one, and in 1928 it was decided to give the church a major overhaul. It was at this time that Joseph Benoit of Nancy was commissioned to produce all

St. Matthew's Brigade, formed in 1909 (Courtesy of Mike Edmunds)

the stained glass windows of the church, and it was also decided to replace the original bell, Madeleine Geneviève Denise (which had initially been made for the original Sacré Cœur chapel at Montmartre) with three new bells. This proved to be a taxing operation. The belfry needed considerable reinforcement with concrete in order to be able to house the weight of the bells; the work was started on April 22nd 1929 under the direction of local architect Mr. Quérée and was carried out by Auguste Amourette. The installation of the bells was supervised by Cornille Havard of Villedieu-les-Poëles in Normandy, and the whole operation took more than three months to complete. In the meantime, the interior of the church was totally redecorated, and the workmen were assisted by the Saint-Méen nuns from the Convent. Three new pews were added for the Children of Mary and carpets were purchased from Voisins. The installation of the stained glass by Joseph Benoit had involved intense work, as all the windows of the church were being replaced. The three new bells for the church were blessed on August 11th 1929 although the dates inscribed on the bells indicate the blessing ceremony took place on September 29th. This was because the godmother of the larger of the three bells, Miss MacFeely, could not attend on September 29th, the date chosen to mark the 25th anniversary of Père Pitard's priesthood. The large bell, weighing 385kg was baptized Marie-Joseph, and was donated by Miss MacFeely as well as Dr. Charles Renfrie Chichester of Woodville, St. Peter. The second bell (267kg) was christened Constance-Aline in memory of two Rectors of St. Matthew's, Père Constant Le Vacon and Père Alain Mao. Its godparents were Mr. Alfred Pinel and Mrs Ada Morel. The third bell (195kg) was named Anne-Antoinette in honour of the two patron saints representing the two chapels in the Parish, St. Anne and St. Anthony, and this bell's godparents were Mr. Rémi Deffains and Mrs. Marie Derrien. The three bells were rung for the first time on August 14th, the day before the Feast of Assumption.

A Field in St. Peter

In July 1929, the same Dr. Chichester (and his wife) who had contributed towards the large bell at St. Matthew's, donated a 7-vergée field at Le Clos de Chemin Vert in St. Peter for a chapel. However, it had not been made clear whether the land was actually given to the Diocese of Portsmouth or the Oblates. It emerged on December 9th 1929 in a letter sent by Dr. Chichester to Père Mao that his wish was for the land to belong to the Oblates on three conditions which he hoped would be fulfilled: his desire was for the new chapel to be dedicated to the Immaculate Conception; an altar in the new chapel should be dedicated to St. Benedict (*Saint Benoît* in French); that an annual Mass would be held for himself, his wife and his children. He further stipulated that should the Oblates ever leave Jersey, the value of this field should be given to the Superior General of the Oblates for the money to be used elsewhere by the Order. After a few legal complications, the land was duly given to them in April 1930.

Shortly after the all-important Corpus Christi that year, initial plans were drawn up by the architect Mr. Nicolle who accompanied Père Pitard and the visiting Oblate Provincial, Père Grenier to the field, which by now constituted 10 vergées (another area of land having been added to the first by Dr. Chichester). The plan was to build a large 72-ft building which in due course could be used as a school, thus leaving space for a more formal chapel to be constructed at a later date. Ultimately, these plans did not materialise, and an entry in the *Codex* of August 2nd 1939 refers to the field still being empty. Nevertheless, it was used on a regular basis for fêtes and bazaars, and the annual afternoon tea-party took place there in 1939. In the end, a small wooden chapel was built on a concrete platform in 1946, leaving the rest of the field vacant; the chapel was duly named the Immaculate Conception as requested by Dr. Chichester, and was officially opened on the Feast of the Immaculate Conception, December 8th 1946.[30]

St. Anne's Chapel Repurchased

In 1933, Père Pitard of St. Matthew's was named Superior of Novices and Bursar to a French seminary, and was replaced by Père Jean Louis Messager, a former assistant priest at St. Thomas'. The latter, along with Père Jaïn, dearly wanted to improve facilities at St. Anne's Chapel, and in the final months of 1938, they worked towards repurchasing the old school-chapel in St. Ouen in George Farrell's fields. Bazaars and garden fêtes were held in order to raise money, and thanks to the determination of Père Jaïn and Mrs Eugène (Ada) Morel, the stage was reached whereby an agreement was made with Mgr Cotter to purchase the property; with the additional financial backing of Mlle Mathilde Marie Adelus, the contract was signed at the Royal Court on March 25th 1939. Although only half of the cost was met at this time, a bond was signed by which Mr Farrell would receive the rest of his payment over the coming years along with a £30 interest per annum.

Père Messager employed Peter Rolland, a local carpenter from Grantez in St. Ouen, who promised he could refurbish the property and have it ready to serve as new chapel by Easter that year. True to his word, the chapel was officially inaugurated on Good Friday – April 7th 1939 – with the installation of the Stations of the Cross and a sermon by Père Messager. Over the coming months, various donations and gifts were received at the new chapel – these included Madeleine Geneviève Denise, the former bell from St. Matthew's, and a new harmonium, a gift from Père Legrand. In July 1939 Bishop Cotter paid an official visit to the new St. Anne's Chapel.

In June-July that year the old wooden chapel was dismantled and transported to Ville à L'Evêque where it was re-assembled and transformed into new clubrooms for the local patronages.

Bagatelle Closes

During the early years of the 1920s the FCJ Sisters had received a lot of "bad press" in the Catholic neighbourhood as a result of the feud with the French Oblates caused by the sale of schools and above all the Convent at St. Matthew's. This had by no means affected their relations with many of the other Catholic orders in Jersey, and in many respects their endeavours since their arrival in Jersey were regarded by many as a dynamic and bold attempt to unite Christians of all denominations whilst still upholding the Catholic credo.

In 1926, it was decided that if the success of their school in Jersey should continue, all emphasis should be placed on the main convent-school at David Place and Vauxhall Elementary. Funding was low. Although it was the Bishop of Portsmouth who had sent the Sisters to Jersey in the first place, the expenses of their upkeep as well as salaries for teaching staff fell exclusively on the Sisters. The school at Bagatelle was therefore shut down and sold to Jerseyman Robert Henry Miller in 1927.

St. Aubin's – A New Church

Père Alain Mao had been longing for a new church in St. Aubin's since his early days at the beginning of the 1900s when he was given the responsibility of St. Aubin's district. On the back of a postcard found amongst his belongings depicting a church in France which resembled the (as yet unplanned) new church for his district, he had written: "This is the church I would like to build at St. Aubin's!" By 1912 he had developed a positive working relationship with the architect Julien Barbier, and they drew up plans for a flamboyant neo-gothic style church.

As Père J.B. Lemius, the former Superior at Montmartre, wrote in the obituary for Père Mao, the main reason why a new church was not built soon after the initial plans had been made was quite simply because he knew Père Mao wanted the church to be a masterpiece:

> Why didn't he start building the church? Indeed he could have easily built it if he had wanted a chapel or an ordinary church. But he wanted it to be **beautiful**, worthy of the Sacred Heart, worthy of the Island of Jersey.[31]

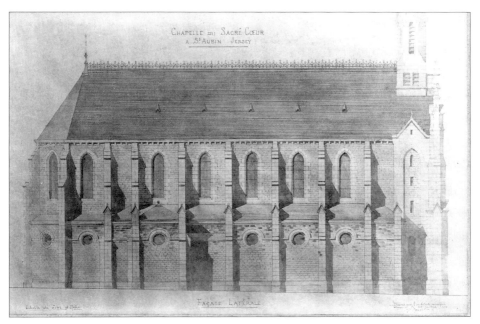

Architect Julien Barbier's original 1912 design for the Sacred Heart Church at St. Aubin (Courtesy of St. Thomas' Church)

Bishop Cotter blessing the foundation stone at the Sacré Cœur Church, St. Aubin, November 1st 1937 (Courtesy of St. Thomas' Church)

He felt such a fondness for the district that he managed to arrange for it to be part of "his" Parish, whether he was Rector as St. Matthew (1919-1920) or Superior at St. Thomas', a post he occupied for the following thirteen years. He devoted his life to collecting funds for the "beautiful church" he dreamed of. Even in his final years he persevered for the building of the church, working from the Sacré Cœur Orphanage where he now lived alongside Père Legrand, collecting money as he had done for 30 years, and travelling each day from St. Helier to St. Aubin. It was only in 1936 when his health was failing that he stopped travelling there on a daily basis, but he knew by then that his plans would materialise, even though he was aware that he would not actually live to witness his dream. He died on February 3rd 1937, a matter of months before the foundation stone was laid by Bishop Cotter, on November 1st 1937. Although the ultimate design for the new church was not as grandiose as he had originally dreamed of back in 1912, the architecture of the church was still worthy of the "beautiful" homage to the Sacred Heart he had strived for all those years.

Building work commenced immediately, and the church should have been completed by 1939, but the outbreak of World War II that year interrupted the final stages of the work, and by the time it was ready to be opened by Mgr King of Portsmouth, on June 8th 1947, the French Oblates, who had been aware of the increase in the number of English-speaking parishioners for some time, had decided to hand over the new Parish of St. Aubin's to the Anglo-Irish Oblates of Jersey the previous year. However, the first Rector of the new Sacred Heart Parish was the French Oblate Père Louis Jean-Marie Julien Choinel who began holding Mass at the church during the Occupation years.

IV

War

8 The German Occupation

The outbreak of World War II on September 1st 1939 affected all Islanders. Rumours of war in the summer had already led to hotels being vacated and crops abandoned; even the discovery of the Colorado Beetle faded into insignificance alongside the reality of imminent war. Gas masks were distributed to Islanders and blackout was the order of the day. In June 1940 with the demilitarisation of Jersey, 23,000 people left in two days, and as a consequence, many of the Island's schools found themselves very low in numbers. A large number of Jersey's buildings were taken over by the German military, food became scarce, Islanders were being deported and interned, hardship was affecting everyone, and the inhabitants of the Island found themselves in a position whereby solidarity became the *leitmotiv* for the duration of the Occupation irrespective of religious denomination. In many respects, the five years of Occupation drew Catholics and Protestants closer to each other; and internal squabbles virtually disappeared. A huge community spirit evolved. An analysis of a number of reports and diaries belonging to various churches in Jersey which chart the War years shows that there was a significant decrease in negative remarks with regards to (a) other faiths and (b) internal disputes.[1]

Volumes could be written about the numerous incidents and stories which occurred during the Occupation and which have been recalled by members of the Catholic community in Jersey and by those individuals who were forced to leave the Island, a task which no doubt will be fulfilled at a later stage, but for the purpose of this book, we shall limit ourselves to charting a broader outline of events which marked Catholic life during those years.

The FCJ Schools

The Annals of the Faithful Companions of Jesus provide a very vivid insight into the events surrounding the Occupation of Jersey and the effect this had on the schools.

> With the first air bombardment the Sisters went to the school basement and went back to the refectory two hours later to finish their supper. Like everyone else in the Island they sought shelter several times that first weekend. Then came the German parachutist to announce "takeover" in two days time by when all were to have white flags flying from their windows. Calico cost 6d a yard so "old garments" were pressed into use for twelve small and two large windows whilst 2,100 panes of glass had to be crossed with paper. Rationing was strict and the Sisters faced another problem in that shopkeepers were now asking for cash payment. The June Sale of Work had to be cancelled and the community thought ruefully of the accumulation of plain and fancy needlework which remained unsold.[2]

The records of the FCJ Sisters give us a graphic picture of what life was like during the Occupation, and they also reveal how, like most Islanders, they had to think ahead in order to "outwit" the enemy. Mère Marie Hélène Laverrie, a past pupil of Bagatelle, was Superior between 1940 and 1946. At the first rumour of invasion she and Mother Philomena Ayers decided to spend all available cash on food, and they gathered together as many tinned cans as they could:

> I had an inspiration. I would hide the tinned food under the platforms on which stood the teachers' desks. All our work was done at night and very soon all the tinned goods were hidden. We still had dry goods, matches, shoe polish and so on to hide. Fortunately there were many cupboards in the house and it was amusing for me to find hiding places for all the goods. Some survived the war and were found in peace time.
>
> Although I could rely on the community, it would have been foolish to tell them. Instead, I simply asked them not to move the teachers' desks on any account. Mother Philomena, the headmistress, Sister Aloysius (Hall) who was in charge of cleaning

the school and myself were the only ones who knew where things were hidden. I kept many things to myself so that if any of the Sisters were questioned they could answer without hesitation "I don't know."[3]

In spite of reduced numbers, the school continued to function, but changes were noticed by all, teachers and pupils. German language had to be taught four hours a week to every child over the age of ten, and surprise inspections were commonplace. Mère Marie Hélène refers to one such inspection in her notes, when a German officer arrived at David Place in order to find out how much German language had been acquired by the pupils.

> We were lucky to have Mother Gertrude Collins who had lived in Germany when she was young and who spoke the language fluently. The children had been well taught and knew many German songs. I welcomed the inspector and asked him to come to the hall for the assembly, and explained that the whole school would be there. Mother Dolores Haughey soon had the girls singing German songs, and on and on they went until the Inspector exclaimed "They sing like little Fräulein!" and then asked to be shown round the school...We never had another visit.[4]

Certain privations affected their religious life – the Annals inform us that the supply of altar breads became very low, and by 1944 the Sisters were only able to receive communion three times a week until they could find means to make more hosts. We are also informed that the pupils were encouraged to share whatever they could, and aware of the fact that the Carmelites living at Hautmont were particularly needy during the Occupation, they donated the sum of £12 after a fund-raising event in 1943.

The Convent Chaplain during the Occupation was Father Stephen Bernard Campbell, and it was he who composed the Mass which was sung at St. Thomas' on V-J Day. He died on November 7th 1945 and was buried at Almorah.

De La Salle College

1940 was a hard year for the College: the number of Brothers was reduced from six to three. One of the three who left, was a German national, Brother Carl Franz, and although many people in authority tried to intercede for him, he was interned. The impact of the War was felt strongly by all, and the number of pupils decreased sharply – from 230 at the start of the year to 164 by December.[5] The School Chaplain, Father Hargreaves, had had to leave the Island along with the evacuees, and during the Occupation Mass was held by Belgian Jesuit Fathers who had fled to Jersey in May 1940 when Belgium had been invaded by the Germans and were now based at Maison Saint-Louis. As contact was lost with England during the Occupation, the pupils could no longer sit Matriculation examinations, and as a consequence local examinations were set up in the hope that these would be validated by the English boards at a later date.

The school records indicate the sadness felt by teachers and pupils alike at the news they received of the death of 73-year-old Mgr Cotter, Bishop of Portsmouth, on October 24th 1940. A dynamic man who had been Bishop for 35 years, Mgr Cotter had frequently visited Jersey's Catholic community and had played a key role in the development of many areas of their life.

The main problems we read of in the school's reports for the War years were failing health amongst pupils and teachers, and the general lack of teaching staff. In 1942 two young English Brothers from Highlands were welcomed to the school to help out, but within a day they were removed from the Island and sent to a concentration camp. Sports events had to be cancelled, as the pupils were not strong enough to compete. Uncertainty, coupled with the loss of Old Boys and friends of the school killed in action or interned in Germany (the latter including the school gardener Marcel Gicquel), added to a sense of despair as the War progressed. By the time the School Chronicle for 1943-44 was written, there was the feeling that

> ..loyalty, enthusiasm, piety, punctuality, application to study, even interest in games showed an extraordinary decline due no doubt to the long drawn-out War.[6]

Maison Saint-Louis and Bon Secours College

In July 1946, just over a year after the end of the War, The *Chronique des Frères de l'Instruction Chrétienne de Ploërmel*, mouthpiece for the Ploërmel Brothers, started to publish a series of articles which ultimately spanned about 25 pages and a number of issues; these articles give us detailed information regarding their years in Jersey during the German Occupation, a chronicle of events providing us with a very powerful insight into the conditions at Bon Secours College and various episodes which coloured their existence.

On June 22nd 1940, the Highlands community received a telephone call from the French Consul asking them if they would be prepared to put up a group of forty French soldiers who had escaped the Germans at Cherbourg and had managed to reach the Island. This was the beginning of the Brothers' involvement in five years of Occupation.

On July 1st 1940, the German forces arrived in Jersey; and for the first few months, despite rationing and major changes in Island life, life was able to continue as normal at the College:

> The first few months of the Occupation were relatively calm. From the outset, there was moderate rationing on meat, flour, sugar, butter, tobacco etc. Cabarets, theatres and dance halls were shut down. The use of private vehicles and sale of petrol were forbidden, as was listening to English radio; it seemed harsh, but was nothing compared to what was to come next. Admittedly the town's streets were full of German soldiers, but once one had left the perimeters, there were virtually none to be seen. [...]
>
> At Bon Secours we felt very peaceful; the lack of cabarets, cars and radios didn't bother us at all.[7]

However, things rapidly changed. On August 3rd there was a raid at Maison Saint-Louis, the Germans keen to question the Jesuit Fathers. Some were deported. Numbers dwindled significantly at Maison Saint-Louis, and within months there were only ten Jesuit Fathers remaining. A few months later, at the end of January 1941, the Brothers at Bon Secours received an order written in German, demanding that all the French students return immediately to France. They were to take blankets and provisions and plan their departure at once. This order caused some mild panic amongst the students and Brothers, who feared the students might meet an untoward fate on their arrival in France; as it emerged, those who did leave were better off than those who either had to stay and face even stricter rationing, or worse still, those (like the English Brothers) who were interned in Germany. On February 18th the first group from Bon Secours left the Island: thirty-nine scholastics and two Brothers, each carrying a 24-hour supply of food and water, a few books, and some blankets. Fifty-two novices, their teacher and a few other Brothers left by boat to Granville in the same way as the previous group on February 21st. This left a matter of twenty Brothers at Bon Secours. The Chapel was closed and St. Joseph's House was transformed into a temporary chapel.

Like so many others, Père Boutrolle, the Chaplain of the College, had been called back to France, and his role was filled by the 75-year-old Jesuit priest from Maison Saint-Louis, Père Joseph Paul Marie de Tonquédec who faithfully held Mass at the makeshift chapel in St. Joseph's House every single day. The author of the articles points out that on occasions, German Catholic soldiers would come to Mass, and not a glimmer of hostility was felt on either side.

Rationing became stricter, but this did not affect the Brothers to start with. In the months leading up to the Occupation, the Brothers had taken similar precautions to the FCJ Sisters, and had amassed food and supplies, and these lasted a considerable time as a large number of College members had to leave the Island. Furthermore, the Brothers had the privileged advantage of having large grounds and an impressive kitchen garden where they still employed boys from the Orphanage to help out. As the war crisis developed, all became involved in the gardening effort; they were also fortunate in having a neighbour who could no longer export his produce to the British mainland, and he frequently donated vegetables to the Brothers.

An order of French nuns from Broons in Brittany, *Les Filles de Sainte-Marie de la Présentation*, often referred to as *Les Sœurs de Broons*,[8] had been resident at Bon Secours College for a number of years. These nuns had come to assist the Brothers with household chores, and during the Occupation three of them remained at Bon Secours. They also played an active role in assuring the well-being of the whole Highlands community.

During the summer of 1941, major changes occurred which were to colour the Brothers' existence for the duration of the War. The

Germans, aware that England had not fallen, feared a British attack on the Channel Islands, and began to build massive fortifications which involved bringing an extra 10,000 German troops to Jersey. According to some reports, as many as 25,000 were deployed, amounting to more than half of Jersey's actual population at the time. Additionally, many foreign prisoners of war, particularly Russians, were brought to Jersey to work as forced labour. In order to accommodate all these new soldiers, many buildings and large houses in Jersey were taken over and occupied by the Germans. Bon Secours College was no exception. With most of the students now back in France, the buildings were more or less empty apart from the twelve Brothers remaining, and on June 20th 1941, 180 German soldiers arrived and spent the night there. Initially, the Brothers assumed this was going to be a temporary measure; ultimately their buildings were occupied for four years. The buildings were divided up amongst the Germans and the Brothers, the latter being left St. Joseph's House, half of Bon Secours College, the gardens and a refectory. At Maison Saint-Louis similar arrangements were made by the occupying forces, although it is understood they were less than satisfied with the dilapidated state of the main building, and attempted to refurbish it themselves. During the latter part of the War, Maison Saint-Louis was used by the Germans for the training of NCOs.

The new arrangements did not affect their daily life too much. Brick walls and fences had been erected to partition off various parts of Bon Secours College, and although there were up to 400 Germans living there, this did not disturb their existence. It was the unexpected which came as a shock, such as the expulsion of a young Haitian Brother in April 1942, followed by the more brutal expulsion of the two 18-year-old English Brothers whom they had willingly sent to De La Salle College to help out the reduced staff level. On September 16th that year, over 2000 English residents of the Channel Islands were expelled from the Islands and sent to various camps in Germany.

As the War progressed and the final years became harder for all Islanders, the Brothers too shared a feeling of isolation and despair. They were cut off from the rest of the world, with no radio contact, and were forbidden from enjoying the simple aspects of Jersey life, such as walking on the beach, sketching landscapes, staying out late in the evening etc... and as Frère Joseph Libert, the author of the

November 1946 article in the *Chronique des Frères* points out:

> The Islanders were suffering a lot, and their most painful sufferings were not caused by lack of bread or shoes.
> A major part of this suffering was firstly the prolonged isolation, the lack of news and correspondence for five long years, and secondly the unremitting hammering of Nazi propaganda.... At first, we used to possibly laugh at their fantasies and yarns. But when you hear it all over and over again you almost start to believe it, you get upset by it, shattered by it, thrown into confusion, discouraged.[9]

This was not helped by the fact that the immense feeling of hope in June 1944, brought about by the Normandy Landings, was shattered when Islanders realised that the War was not over.

> For a long time, we hoped that this event would signal an end to the Occupation. What an empty illusion: the Germans stayed on. Jersey was cut off, there was no communication, no way to bring in any supplies. During the winter which followed, the sense of despair reached a new level.[10]

There was no gas supply, and the Island had run out of candles. In the chapel at St. Joseph's House, they made use of the final candles they had remaining, and ultimately reduced themselves to cutting up the hosts for communion, so that one host would cover several people.

Finally, on May 9th 1945, the Channel Islands were liberated. At Maison Saint-Louis, the property was immediately taken over by British troops. The day after the Islands were liberated, on May 10th (which was also Ascension Day), the Brothers at Bon Secours College were finally able to open up those parts of the building which had been occupied by the German forces. Although the damage caused in the property was not as bad as they had anticipated, a lot of repair work was needed before the College could resume as normal. The electricity had to be restored and over 200 window panes needed replacing. It was only two years after the end of the War, in March 1947 that the first group of English and French students arrived at the College; by Easter 1947, they had 73 students.

The Observatory

Practically the only resident permitted to have a radio set in Jersey during the Occupation was Père Charles Rey at the Maison Saint-Louis Observatory. Allowed to have the wireless for the sole purpose of his research and for setting the correct time on the Island's clocks, Père Rey is known to have taken an active role in the "underground" Resistance movement in Jersey. A gifted scientist, he is understood to have made tiny matchbox crystal radios which he and a number of colleagues were able to use clandestinely in order to find out what the BBC was reporting regarding the state of the War. Many Islanders with wartime memories recall Père Rey's enthusiasm and tenacity.

The Orphanage

Although the Orphanage itself was not occupied during the War, many German soldiers visited the property on frequent occasions, in particular the Summerland Knitting Factory, where they ordered clothing to be made. Sister Peter, in her memoirs, recalls how on one occasion the German Field Commandant Knackfuss arrived at the factory where she was working at a sewing machine. He had come there, not to order any garments, but to inspect the premises. Her own act of defiance and solidarity, to both the French and British, was to discreetly change the cotton bobbins on her machine, so that her enthusiastic sewing produced fabric adorned in red, white and blue. Knackfuss did not notice a thing. As he then inspected the rest of the premises including the Chapel, he was neither aware of the fact that the Sisters had concealed their stock of sugar in religious statues!

St. Thomas's Church

Sister Peter recalls German officers coming to Mass at the Orphanage Chapel, and like most Jersey Catholics who attended Mass at St. Thomas's Church, she has clear recollections of the German Mass which was sung at the "Cathedral" each Sunday at 9 a.m. In fact, all those who were interviewed for this book and who remember the War years, mentioned the same thing: how the German soldiers' singing was incomparable to anything they had heard before. It was of such a high quality and so beautiful to listen to that many local churchgoers would attend the German Mass simply to hear the singing and listen to the organ being played.

The German troops had come to the Island with their own priests and organist. One observer, Andrée Etienne, who later became organist herself at St. Thomas', commented that the sheer power of the German organist's playing would make the instrument almost impossible for Père Théodule Maré to use afterwards when he was celebrating Mass, and that often the harmonium would have to be encouraged quite wildly with the bellows before it deigned to produce a decent note.

St. Matthew's Church and Convent

Both the presbytery and the Convent were occupied by the Germans during the Occupation. We know from records that a number of the French Oblates living in Jersey were recalled to France to serve in the army. These included Père Yves Jaïn who had devoted so much time to oversee the development of St. Anne's Church. Père Jaïn left the Island in September 1939.[11]

With the influx of more German soldiers in Jersey in order to start building the massive fortifications which began to dominate the seaboard and countryside, the presbytery was taken over, and the remaining priests had to find alternative accommodation. They were given shelter at Glencoe Cottage at Carrefour Selous, a property which belonged to Hedley William Maillard. The Saint-Méen Sisters living in the Convent were likewise obliged to find a place to live and work from. Although the Convent was just across the road from the Church, it was just within the boundaries of St. Mary's, and the *Connétable* of the parish came to the Sisters' aid, providing them and Mme Olympe du Feu with a house named Glenside Lodge situated at Bel Royal in St. Lawrence. The ladies were therefore able to resume their teaching at Glenside for the duration of the Occupation. Once the War was over, they all moved back into the Convent.

St. Patrick's Church

Although this project did not involve the French Catholics in Jersey, it is of significance that a new Anglo-Irish Catholic church was actually opened in the Island during the War. Midway through the German

Occupation, two Catholics who regularly worshipped at St. Mary's and St. Peter's – Bob Troy and Fred Knight – decided to transform a former army hut at Samarès (which had been turned into a couple of small cottages) into the new church. An altar was loaned to the church by De La Salle College, and many generous donors helped to equip the building which was opened in 1943 within the octave of St. Patrick, a fitting date for a church for which the name of Ireland's patron saint had already been chosen.[12]

The Sacred Heart Church, St. Aubin

St. Aubin's

Père Louis Choinel, the French Oblate priest who became the first Rector of the Sacré Cœur Parish and who played a major role in the building of the new Church of the same name, is remembered by many Islanders for having held services in the new building during the Occupation, even though the Church itself was not officially opened until 1947.[13] Until the new church was used, services were still held at the old church hall on Mont les Vaux which was also used as a Catholic social club. During the War years, the new Sacré Cœur Church was often regarded by many observant and informed Islanders as a secret religious symbol of Resistance. Barely visible on the granite frontage of the church, half-way up between the porch and the belfry, is a ship's anchor, ingeniously integrated into the general design work; the stonemason responsible for this anchor (which did not feature in any of Julien Barbier's plans for the church, or in the contractor Charles Le Quesne's records) was the Breton-born Roman Catholic Joseph Le Guyader, who had been continuing the work on the church in spite of there only being a skeleton staff available. The story of how the anchor became an integral part of the new church's design only became public many years later, in 1956, by which time Joseph Le Guyader was long since dead. However, for those who knew Le Guyader in 1940 when he undertook this risky act of defiance, the church had a new symbol attached to it.

When the Le Guyader family spoke of Joseph's decision to incorporate an anchor into the stonework, they explained the entire background for his choice of motif: on December 18th 1939, one of Hitler's prized battleships, the Admiral Graf Spee, was scuttled in a major British naval victory off the coast of Montevideo in South America. The impact of the War at the end of 1939 being far from encouraging, this piece of news acted as a positive catalyst for many Islanders, and the "underground" knowledge that a symbol for this German defeat / British naval victory was being incorporated into the body of a new place of worship, effectively became a morale-booster.[14] Additionally, it can be noted that the shape of the anchor traces the contours of a Christian Cross with two upward-pointing arrows in Victory formation.

Père Albert Durand

Although numerous Catholics with Jersey connections met untimely deaths during the War, or alternatively were arrested and interned in Germany or elsewhere, it seems appropriate to mention Père Albert Durand O.M.I. in the context of this book. He was born in Jersey in 1916 and studied with the Jesuits here in the Island before continuing his studies at the Juniorate in Pontmain and the Novitiate at Berder, taking his first vows in 1937. With the outbreak of War he was transferred to Notre-Dame-des-Lumières, trekking across France and ultimately meeting his former master, Père Pitard, in Bordeaux; the same Père Pitard who had been Rector of St. Matthew's between 1920 and 1933. Ordained priest in 1942 he was assigned a parish just outside Lunières where he was arrested by the Gestapo who found a British passport in his suitcase. As he explained in a talk given at the Playhouse Theatre on September 27th 1945, he was accused of being a British agent and was tried as such. After his trial he was classified as a *Nachtung Nebel* prisoner, "a prisoner to all intents and purposes who has disappeared from the face of the earth."[15] He was transported in an overpacked cattle truck to Neubrem where he was imprisoned. He was later moved to Dachau, Natzweiler-Struthof and back to Dachau. The years spent in these traumatic concentration camps took their toll on Père Durand, and as Père Gaston Delaunay reports in the obituary he wrote in 1974, "he was eventually liberated, but his captivity left its indelible mark on his body and spirit and was no doubt somewhat responsible for his brutal death."[16] After a few months spent recuperating in England after his release from Dachau, he returned to Jersey and spent fourteen years (1945-1959) as assistant priest to Père Eugène Méline at St. Martin before moving back to Notre-Dame-de-Sion.

François Scornet (1921-1941)

The Frenchman most Islanders associate with wartime Jersey is the 20-year-old François Scornet, executed at St. Ouen's Manor on March 17th 1941. The story of his final hours was related in *Les Chroniques de Jersey* on August 25th 1945, not by an historian, but by Père Théodule Maré, Superior at St. Thomas', who had given Scornet the last rites, had accompanied him to the Manor and witnessed his death. This was his account:

> On December 13th 1940, sixteen young men secretly left the small fishing harbour of Dourduff near Morlaix, intending to reach England and join General de Gaulle's army. After a rough crossing they arrived in Guernsey thinking it was the Isle of Wight.
> Caught by the Germans, they appeared before a first court-martial on January 3rd 1941. Afterwards they were brought to

Jersey where they were sentenced by the court-martial of the 515 Feldkommandantur. Four of them were condemned to death and the others to lengthy imprisonment.

In the end, only one of them was executed. It was the young François Scornet who was considered to be the main ringleader of the group. On March 16th in the evening, two German officers came to St. Thomas' presbytery and asked to speak to me. They had come to inform me that a Frenchman who had been condemned to death, was going to be executed the following morning. Presuming him to be Roman Catholic they suggested I go and visit him before his execution, if I so wished. As I agreed to do so, it was arranged that a taxi would come and fetch me the following morning. So the next morning, March 17th, at 6 o'clock precisely, a taxi arrived with one of the officers I had met the day before. When I sat next to him he handed me a piece of paper on which was written: "Scornet, François, born on May 25th 1919 in Ploujean. Verdict of February 4th 1941: sentenced to death – wished to join de Gaulle to fight against Germany – led his other comrades. The others have been sentenced to hard labour."

Several minutes later we were at the prison. The gaoler opened the cell door and the condemned prisoner came out into the gallery walk which separates the cells from the interior yard. He looked around in astonishment and then realised suddenly that his last hour had arrived. This was, in any case, pointed out to him as his death sentence was read out to him. I then moved forward, shook his hand, telling him that I was a French Catholic priest. He asked for permission to say farewell to his fifteen friends, and this was granted. [...]

We were then left together in a separate cell for more than half an hour. I had brought the Blessed Sacrament and after devoted preparation the young Breton received Holy Communion from which he drew the strength and courage to persevere to the end of his hard sacrifice, just like the Christian martyrs of the past.

[...]

Meanwhile the moment arrived for us to leave for the place of execution. I was told that my mission was over and that I could retire. I protested and insisted that I wanted to be with the prisoner until the very end. After a few brief exchanges, I was found a seat in one of the cars. When we stopped outside the Grand Hotel I took advantage of the situation to rejoin the condemned man and sit next to him in a four-seater taxi.

From then on, right until the very end, we talked and prayed together. Both the faith and religious fervour of the young Breton were aroused. He lovingly kissed my Oblate Missionary Crucifix, recited and read the wondrous prayers of the Catholic Liturgy.

The cars arrived at the entrance of St. Ouen's Manor just a little before eight o'clock. We got out of the car, and we went along slowly, praying together, walking the three or four hundred yards which separated the main road from the place of execution: a grassy lawn fairly near the manor buildings.

François Scornet was led to the foot of a large tree facing ten soldiers lined up, helmeted and armed, themselves surrounded by a more numerous detachment of other soldiers. To the side, somewhat isolated stood a group of officers. The prisoner was tied around the middle of his body to the tree. I remained constantly by his side. When all the preparations were completed, an officer again read out his sentence condemning him to death – both in German and in French.

François Scornet shouted in a loud and clear voice: Long live God! Long live France! These were his last words in public. I gave him the final absolution and a fraternal embrace, made him kiss my crucifix and moved a few paces away.

A moment later his heart and chest were ripped apart by ten bullets. His body gave a slight start, and then crumpled slowly to the right.[17]

Père Maré gave the dead man a final blessing, and asked the authorities to allow him to bury Scornet at Almorah Cemetery. This was granted providing Scornet was not given any form of religious service in church. His body was taken to the cemetery chapel at Almorah, and a religious burial took place the following day in the presence of the Oblate clergy of St. Thomas', a representative from the prison and a few bystanders. Mr J.B. Le Quesne the undertaker made the necessary arrangements. For several years, wreaths and flowers were brought to Almorah by local Jersey people. Both Père Maré and Père

Jort frequently held Masses praying for the eternal repose of his Christian soul. On the afternoon of the day of the execution, Père Maré returned to the prison and spoke to the remaining fifteen prisoners. A few days later they were sent to prison in Caen. The tree at St. Ouen's Manor was chopped down by the Germans to avoid any local hero-worship.

A few months after the end of the War, on August 24th 1945, his remains were exhumed and were taken to a private chapel at Gas Place belonging to undertakers J.B. Le Quesne and Son; his coffin lay in state covered with a Tricolor until September 18th, when a Requiem Mass was held at St. Thomas' Church;[18] his remains were then transported back to France for reburial in Ploujean, his native village. It was thanks to Fred Langlois who loaned his yacht Callou for this purpose that the coffin of François Scornet was returned to France. The village square in Ploujean has been renamed in Scornet's honour.

François Scornet
(Courtesy of St. Thomas' Church)

V

A Changing World

1945-2007

9 The Schools

Changes at Beaulieu Convent

The War years had left their mark on many of the religious orders in Jersey, and by 1950 it was obvious to the *Auxiliatrices des Ames du Purgatoire* (The Helpers of the Holy Souls) that their work in Jersey had suffered so much as a result of the Occupation, that it would be virtually impossible for them to continue living at such a high cost in Jersey. Besides, they were aware that their services could be put to greater use in countries other than Jersey. In 1950, they decided to leave the Island.

This meant that Beaulieu Convent would be sold; and the Sisters of the Immaculate Conception of Saint-Méen based at St. Matthew's Convent, realising that their current location was not conducive to the development of a productive school in Jersey, spoke to the Oblates about their needs, explaining that it would be more beneficial to the growth of the Catholic school to be based in town than out in the inaccessible countryside. The Rector of St. Matthew's, Père P. Le Bas, understood their position; he also realised that if the Saint-Méen Sisters were to purchase Beaulieu Convent, it would mean the sale of St. Matthew's Convent. Over twenty-five years had passed since the fracas surrounding the previous sale of St. Matthew's, and Père Le Bas knew only too well that much had changed since Père Pitard was Rector of the Parish. The War had raised innumerable questions and taught many lessons: religious interaction between Christian denominations was much greater, but paradoxically, religious congregations of all faiths were dwindling. More people were turning away from the Church and adopting a secular form of life, no longer governed by religion. Theological questioning had invaded people's consciences; the huge impact of the War's destructive hand had heightened the problem of

*Pupils at St. Matthew's Convent School supervised by one of the Sisters of the Immaculate Conception of Saint-Méen-Le-Grand
(Courtesy of Sister Marie-Louise)*

evil in the world, and to his dismay he was aware that some people could no longer find their answers through God or prayer. For many, it was easier to deny God's existence than to search for answers through faith. Both Père Le Bas and his predecessor, Père Jean-Louis Messager who died in 1949, were aware of this, and both lamented the smaller congregations in church. One thing was clear: no longer did it matter whether Protestants bought the old Convent or not. What **did** matter was that the Catholic school should thrive in town. In fact, Père Le Bas was quite adamant that the only way forwards was for the Sisters to purchase Beaulieu Convent and succeed there. The only concern for the Oblates and the Saint-Méen Sisters was that St. Matthew's Convent should not land in the hands of someone who would not respect the heritage of the building. Fortunately for all concerned, the new proprietors were the furniture merchants Fred Langlois and his family, who then used the property for the storage of their wares. Unlike so many buildings of historical value in Jersey which were bulldozed during post-war years, the former Convent is still standing to this day, now the property of David Hick.

The Sisters of the Immaculate Conception of Saint-Méen-Le-Grand purchased Beaulieu Convent, and along with Mme Olympe du Feu (who had co-founded the small school at St. Matthew's), Sr Agnès and the other nuns moved the new school on October 2nd 1950. As French-born Sister Marie-Louise (Headmistress at the Convent between 1958 and 1989), has pointed out, the property they moved into was in great need of repair work. It was obvious that the previous owners, the *Auxiliatrices*, had not had much funding in the final years of their stay in Jersey. Beaulieu Convent was gloomy and dank, and it sorely needed cheering up. The Sisters did as much as they could in the first few months, and by January 1951, the school opened with 16 girls and 18 boys of infant school age. By 1958, when Sister Marie-Louise arrived in Jersey to take over as Headmistress, there were already over 200 pupils. For a number of years, the Sisters, by now known over the Island as the "Beaulieu Sisters" also sent staff down to St. Aubin's where they operated the small school on Mont Les Vaux until this became too complex, both for financial and practical reasons. In town, the new establishment went from strength to strength, and it soon became firmly established as a first-class Catholic school. Sister Marie-Louise retired in 1989. Mrs. Rosemarie Hill became the first lay head, and in 2006 Mr. Chris Beirne became the new Principal – and significantly, the first male head.

Over the years, new blocks and wings have been added to the school, and latest statistics show that it has grown to an establishment of over 630 girls ranging from ages 4 to 18. There are 210 in the primary School and 420 in the Secondary School, which includes a Sixth Form of over 80. In 2000 the school acquired the status of a charitable trust with the Order relinquishing all assets and control.

Convent FCJ

By the end of the War, numbers of pupils at Vauxhall Elementary School had fallen, and since the secondary school at David Place was overflowing, the Superior General, Mother Philomena Higgins, decided that the space occupied by the primary school would be better employed by being made available to the secondary school.[1]

By then, major demographic changes were taking place in Jersey. The Island no longer had the large French community it had had in the past, and the school had fewer French pupils on its registers. Furthermore, the boarding school, kept open until 1966, was closed that year, as more and more of the students were now day pupils not needing any accommodation. Although the times were changing, only the attitude of the States of Jersey towards religious education in schools did not seem to waver with regards to the instruction of religion in schools. During the early 1950s there were many complaints in the press, and rallies attended by Archbishop King of Portsmouth were arranged in 1953, petitioning for the promotion of denominational religious education in all primary schools and for financial grants to aid private schools, but both of these petitions were defeated in the States. It was only in 1964 that a law to help independent schools was passed (even though the original law of 1922 forbidding the States to aid private schools was not repealed!)

Already in the early 1950s, the problem of space and adequate school facilities was high on the FCJs' agenda. It was during this period that the Superior, Mother Eustochium Tyler, purchased Midvale House on behalf of the Order, refurbishing the building so that it could adequately house the growing number of pupils. One of the most memorable features of Midvale House was the 6 ft-high statue of the Sacred Heart which was placed in front of the entrance in 1961. It had been at Val Plaisant since 1925 – the only exhibit to gain a prize in the Salon des Beaux Arts in Paris that year. Initially placed behind the High Altar, it became a great feature of Midvale House.

However, the facilities were not up to the required standards. It was felt that the old Convent at David Place could no longer be used as a school, and Midvale House lacked the space for classrooms, recreation and activities. The FCJ records indicate that dry rot was rampant in 1966. A decision had to be made:

> The Sisters realised that if they were to stay in Jersey the Society would have to purchase land and build two new schools. Negotiations were put in hand to buy Grainville. Bishop Worlock, at Prize Day in 1968, assured his audience that he was fully behind the decision.[2]

By 1969, Grainville Manor and its grounds were purchased, and in January that year the old buildings were demolished to pave the way for a modern convent school, capable of housing a preparatory and secondary school as well as all the outdoor facilities necessary.

Demolition of FCJ Convent Chapel, David Place, 1971
(Copyright © Jersey Evening Post)

In September that year the new Primary School was inaugurated, and almost two years later, the new Senior School and Convent were blessed and officially opened by Cardinal John Carmel Heenan. The old schools were sold to the States. In 1970 Midvale House was demolished for States rental accommodation. A year later, in 1971 the former Convent at David Place, along with its 96-year-old chapel, was likewise demolished in order to build the Convent Court high-rise flats. Not all reactions to these decisions were favourable, and in a Save Jersey's Heritage publication by André Ferrari, *Jersey's Lost Heritage – Fifty Years of Needless Destruction*, the author's comments indicate that the loss of the David Place Convent, Midvale House and Grainville Manor was to be lamented:

Perhaps the saddest loss of the 1970s was the convent of the Faithful Companions of Jesus which dominated Val Plaisant and David Place. Said to be structurally unsound, it was sold to the States and demolished in 1971 for two high-rise blocks of flats. We know now that it could have been converted to another use, even housing, and the fact that so much fine craftsmanship should have been bulldozed is almost beyond belief.[3]

Referring to Grainville Manor, Ferrari continues:

This lovely 18th century manor was demolished to build the *new* FCJ school. The destruction of the manor's fine stonework was merely a prelude to the destruction of the old school in Val Plaisant. Rarely can any school's move have resulted in as much architectural vandalism as this.[4]

Although reactions were mixed, the FCJ Sisters could argue that their new facilities were certainly of a much higher educational standard than the "ramshackle place" they had been living in before.[5] The opening ceremony was highlighted by Cardinal Heenan's address, who praised the beauty of the new school and expressed his pleasure at hearing that the Catholic schools were finally receiving help from the educational authorities.

As from this stage, the three Catholic Secondary schools in Jersey began to run a combined Sixth Form; this enabled students from FCJ, Beaulieu and De La Salle to mix, providing larger discussion groups for all concerned. In the meantime, all three Catholic schools continued petitioning the States of Jersey for a free Catholic primary school in the Island, and in the early 1970s Convent FCJ's suggestion was to phase out the senior school in order to acquire funds to extend the FCJ Primary School so that "as many Catholics as possible may be educated in a Christian environment without paying fees."[6] Ultimately, FCJ Senior School was phased out gradually, and by 1981 it was closed, paving the way for the expansion of the Primary School. The dream for this school to be non-fee paying never came to fruition, and it remains a private school, although compared to a number of other non-Catholic private schools in the Island, the fees are not overwhelmingly high; the school, like all three Catholic schools in Jersey, does receive grant aid from the States of Jersey, and the parents of Catholic children needing financial assistance can receive help through schemes funded by the Order and the Diocese of Portsmouth. In 2002 Sister Cecilia Connolly retired, thus ending 91 years of direct involvement of the Order. Miss Maureen Doyle became the first lay-head at FCJ Primary School in the autumn of that year.

De La Salle College

In 1948 the College was transferred from the French Province of Quimper to the Province of London. In spite of the transfer of province, the same staff was kept on at the College in order to maintain continuity, and it took several years before the school was completely absorbed into the London Province system. The numbers of pupils increased considerably, and it was necessary to expand the buildings, and in the initial stages, the Jesuits at Maison Saint-Louis allowed the College to use some of their classrooms.

Brother Edward, the College's Headmaster for almost 33 years, retired in 1949-50, and returned to Quimper. His influence on the school had been so great that when he died in 1960, the Old Boys sent a delegation to Quimper and made the necessary arrangements for his body to be brought back to Jersey where he was buried in St. Martin's Catholic Cemetery.

During the 1960s a Covenant scheme was introduced which greatly assisted the College's financial future. And in 1976 the States of Jersey agreed to provide the school with generous financial assistance in the form of a capitation grant for running costs. The community of Brothers left the school in August 1995, and Mr. John Sankey became the first lay-head in September that year. The College remains the property of the De La Salle Brothers and is under their trusteeship; one of the Brothers is on the Board of Governors.

Maison Saint-Louis and Observatory

After the War, there were only ten Jesuits remaining at Maison Saint-Louis, these including Père Rey. After having provided housing to German soldiers and British troops, the state of the property was even more precarious than it had been during the Occupation, and although the initial plan was to rehabilitate the house for the return of students, it was ultimately deemed uneconomical and impractical. The French Jesuits in Jersey could also sense that the times were changing, and that a move back to France where they now could continue operating with no governmental threats, would be the wisest decision. Their vast library and most of the furniture was shipped back to France, and the house was put on the market. The Jesuits donated the high altar from their chapel to St. Joseph's Church, Grouville. On May 30th 1953 half the property (the main building) was sold, and shortly afterwards the property once again became a hotel, this time the Hotel de France. Père Rey stayed on at the Observatory, the only Jesuit from Maison Saint-Louis remaining. In 1969, when the Weighbridge Gardens instrument site was removed to allow an extension for the bus station, Père Rey willingly augmented his recording programme and the Observatory became Jersey's official Health Resort station.

The States of Jersey bought the Observatory in 1974, "recognising its importance in terms of a very long series of recordings".[7] Père Rey spent another 5 years in charge of the Observatory until his accident in December 1979, often regarded as an indirect cause of his death in France in March 1981. After Père Rey's departure, the continuity of records was upheld by members of the Meteorological Department at Jersey Airport.

Bon Secours College

In March 1947 Bon Secours College resumed its role as an educational establishment and during the first decade or so, life regained its habitual pace. In 1954 the *Sœurs de Broons* returned to France and were replaced by six nuns from a Spanish order, *Hermanas Del Amor de Dios*, who assisted the Brothers with laundry and kitchen work. However, as the years progressed, the numbers of Brothers began to decline quite radically, and as Eileen Nicolle informs us in her *History of Highlands College*, "they gradually took charge of the sacristy and the altar linen, washing and ironing this daily."[8] By the end of the 1960s there was a serious crisis in recruiting young men for the religious order of Brothers, and in 1970 there was a complete reorganisation of its general administration. The new Superior General was Frère Albert Tremblay. A major decision had to be taken, and ultimately the College was put up for sale. There were a number of interested buyers, including an Anglo-American company which had hopes of creating a "Common Market School", but after much deliberation,[9] the Education Committee decided to purchase the property in 1972, their plan being to establish a College of Further Education as well as a seat for the Education Committee. The contract was signed in September 1972. That summer, even though the final contract of sale had not been passed, the Brothers moved all their belongings out of the property. As the *Chronique des Frères* informs us,

As from the end of June, removals were the order of the day, even though the contract of sale still hadn't been signed by August. After having transported the remains of our dead [back to France] and sending the first container of goods to Béthanie where our novices will be living, the library of our Venerable Father and other books were shipped to Ploërmel: approximately 15,000 volumes and 152 crates.[10]

Bon Secours Cemetery (Highlands) (Courtesy of F.I.C.)

The removals involved sending goods, archives and furniture in three directions: to the motherhouse in Ploërmel, to Rome where the new administrative headquarters and archives would be established, and to L'Institution Béthanie in the town of Ciboure in the French Basque region, where an institute belonging to the Order was situated. As the author of the above article indicates, the Brothers decided that the mortal remains of the Brothers who had died in Jersey should be exhumed from the Bon Secours Cemetery (which had been opened and blessed by Mgr Cotter in 1931). The exhumation ceremony took place at Bon Secours Cemetery on June 7th 1972. Presided by their Chaplain Père Debray, the service took place at the foot of the 29 graves. The following day, funeral directors Pitcher and Le Quesne, accompanied by a doctor, a police officer and two delegates representing the Constables of St. Saviour and St. Helier, began the task of exhuming the bodies. This work was completed on June 13th. On the 16th, a large container of coffins was shipped to St. Malo on the Commodore Goodwill, arriving on June 17th. The remains of the 29 Brothers were then taken to Ploërmel where some of them were re-interred in the cemetery belonging to the Community. Others were buried in Josselin. By the end of September the contracts were all signed and the Brothers and novices left Jersey after having spent exactly a half century in the Island, a place which the Head Archivist in Rome recently referred to in a letter as "our refuge."[11]

The Sacré Cœur Orphanage and Grounds

After World War II, the Sacré Cœur Orphanage continued to play a major role in Catholic life in Jersey; in fact, the whole complex can be regarded a hub of activity. St. Thomas' Sports Club, and later St. Thomas' Church Club used the premises at St. Mary's House as meeting place and games hall, and the *Salle des Fêtes* prospered as a theatre and danceroom. Religious ceremonies would take place in the extensive grounds of the Orphanage, and the annual Corpus Christi procession staged its open air Mass there, an event which attracted thousands of Catholics. Sports days and summer fêtes would also take place in the grounds. St. Mary's House, cared for and run by the Sisters since the priests left the premises, was later used for a while by workers, mainly Portuguese nationals who were employed at the Sangan

Summerland Factory.

Many locals have confirmed that the role of the whole of the Sacré Cœur complex was crucial to the practical wellbeing of an overwhelming number of Catholics based in Jersey, especially those who were struggling financially. Whilst the churches offered religious solace, the Sacré Cœur was the "heart and warmth" of Jersey Catholic life, providing many with a dynamic Christian spirit of generosity; and as Pat Lucas, who lived with her mother at St. Mary's House, underlined when discussing her own memories of the post-war Orphanage, it was the unique atmosphere of selfless giving which gave the place its own aura, one which she claimed almost pre-empted the very essence of the Second Vatican Council.

However, by the late Sixties, the need for an orphanage became less apparent; additionally, certain religious events were being reduced in size – the Corpus Christi procession ceased to take place on such a scale, and much to the distress of the Sisters, financial difficulties crept in which forced them to sell part of the property. Large areas of the grounds were sold to various local businesses for development and construction. St. Mary's House was sold to the States in the early 1980s and became the site for the Police Station car park, the Ambulance Station and new houses. The Orphanage itself evolved into a nursery which was still run by the Sisters, and in 1973 was registered by the Education Committee as a Day Nursery. The *Salle des Fêtes*, used for a number of years for jumble sales, enjoyed a brief revival as a theatre until the early 1990s, although this too did not survive the economic pressure and changing times. By 1996 the Sacré Cœur Nursery was obliged to close and the property was sold.[12] When asked directly, many Islanders agreed that this closure without doubt signalled the final decline of the French Catholic presence in Jersey.

Our Lady, Queen of the Universe, Millbrook
photographed in January 2007

10 The Churches

St. Aubin's Parish

It was two years after the end of World War II that the new Sacred Heart Church at St. Aubin's was finally officially opened and blessed by Bishop John Henry King of Portsmouth. Shortly after the end of the War, the French Oblates decided to hand over the new Parish to the Anglo-Irish Oblates – Père Choinel was thus the only French Rector of the Parish, even though he was a fluent English-speaker and had previously been based in British Colombia as a missionary. It was Father Donal Murphy O'Connor of the Anglo-Irish Province who became the new Rector on September 29th 1946; an article in the *Jersey Evening Post* of October 1st 1946 refers to Bishop King paying a special visit to Jersey for this occasion.

In 1947, the Church records also indicate that a new place of worship had been opened at La Moye in St. Brelade; over the following two decades this small chapel, dedicated to St. Theresa and manned by the Anglo-Irish Oblates, underwent various changes and developments until it was closed down in the summer of 1972. In 1968 it re-housed a number of the religious artifacts from the small Immaculate Conception "Airport" chapel which had been obliged to close in the autumn of 1968, and which was finally demolished in November that year as part of the runway extension scheme at Jersey Airport. This included the small Lourdes-style grotto which had been added to the chapel. By September 1972, the new central church of St. Bernadette's at Quennevais was nearing completion; the aim of this modern edifice was to replace both St. Theresa's at La Moye and also the lost Airport Chapel. St. Bernadette's was opened and blessed by Bishop Derek John Worlock on September 10th 1972.

Another church opened in the west of Jersey and soon became part of the Sacred Heart Parish: Our Lady, Queen of the Universe (originally served from St. Mary's and St. Peter's using the First Tower Institute) was built at Millbrook in 1956. During the last two decades of the twentieth century, however, church attendance dwindled considerably; additionally, fewer people were becoming priests, economical difficulties had set in, and by the early years of the twenty-first century it became clear to the Catholic Church in Jersey that the only option would be to sell the building. It was closed down in the autumn of 2003 and was sold to property developers. The large figure of Christ on the front of the building, originally donated by Fred Langlois, was removed and transported to St. Mary's and St. Peter's Church in Wellington Road.

St. Matthew's Parish

With an increase in the number of English-speaking parishioners in Jersey after the War, it was decided that St. Matthew's Parish should also be handed over to the Anglo-Irish Oblates. Père Le Bas, whose last *Codex* entry is from 1952, was the last French priest of the Parish, and he was succeeded that same year by Father Teddy Maher.

While St. Matthew's Church continued to thrive as the hub of activity in the Parish, the two remaining annexes forming part of the Parish – St. Anne's in St. Ouen and Ville à L'Evêque at Trinity – ultimately succumbed to the economical pressure which was overtaking the Catholic Church. St. Anne's closed down in 1985. The church and land were sold for housing developments and the church itself demolished. Much later, in 2004, the church at Ville à L'Evêque was put on the market for similar reasons; however, it was agreed that the church would not follow the same fate as St. Anne's, and it would be developed into a house, leaving the actual building intact. The stained-glass windows were removed from the church and are now the property of St. Thomas' Church.

St. Martin's Parish

St. Martin's Parish remained under the direction of the French Oblates until 1960. Between the end of the War and the Anglo-Irish takeover, a number of significant enhancements were made to the various churches within the Parish. Shortly after the Occupation, the wooden altar in

St. Martin's Church was replaced with a stone altar. This was a gift from the Sacré Cœur Orphanage. Until it came to St. Martin's Church it had been an integral part of the chapel at St. Mary's House, the former Oblate Juniorate. Made in Angers by Rouillard and Co., it had originally been consecrated by Mgr Augustin Dontenwill, Superior General of the Oblates, in 1923.[1] It was reconstructed in St. Martin's and consecrated by Bishop King of Portsmouth on March 22nd 1949.

That same year, the bell, cast at Villedieu by Paul Havard in 1865 and which had been in the belfry since that date, had to be melted down and remade. This was undertaken by an English firm, Gillet and Johnston of Croydon. It was blessed and reinstalled on Palm Sunday, April 10th 1949, by Père Pierre Jort, Superior of St. Thomas', and was rung for the first time on Maundy Thursday. Its godparents were Joseph Boléat and Rose Guégan.

In Gorey, it was felt that the small chapel in Gorey Village was not sufficient for the growing population of the area, so in 1953, Père Eugène Aimé Méline bought a property named Badminton Hall in the village; the building had previously been a non-conformist chapel and then a cinema. He arranged for it to be completely refurbished, and on December 20th 1953 the new church was opened. It was blessed by Bishop King on September 26th 1954 and named Our Lady of the Assumption.

At Grouville, St. Joseph's Church also underwent a number of changes. Firstly, the plain glass windows were replaced with stained glass. This was another of Père Méline's initiatives, a project he completed through parishioners' generosity. Another development at St. Joseph's after the Occupation was the installation of the former High Altar from Maison Saint-Louis: this was given to the church by the Jesuits upon their departure from Jersey in remembrance of the years of commitment they had given the district, in particular the thriving social club at the former school. The new Clubroom, a former army hut, was offered to Père Bernard Morin as a testimony of his work as chaplain to the German prisoners of war. On October 1st 1954, St. Joseph's received a new bell, Jeanne-Marie, donated by Mr. Denis Bérézai, a resident of the parish. The name of the bell was chosen in order to commemorate the centenary of the proclamation of the dogma of the Immaculate Conception and also in memory of the golden jubilee of Bishop John Henry King's ordination as priest. That same year, a

Interior of St. Joseph's Church, 1953 (Courtesy of Cecil Rebours)

new altar to Our Lady was placed in the side chapel at St. Joseph's.

On September 8th 1952 Père Méline, Rector of the Parish, celebrated the fiftieth anniversary of his priesthood, and a year later, on October 15th 1953 he decided to retire from Jersey and move back to Notre-Dame-de-Sion. He was replaced by Père Constant Quinton who established a bilingual Parish magazine, *Le Lien*, and made considerable developments to the social club at St. Martin's, converting two rooms into a billiard hall and adding a rifle range to the facilities. Père Quinton retired as Rector on 1957, and the last French Oblate to serve St. Martin's was Père P. Hélouët who handed over the task of running the Parish to the Anglo-Irish Oblate priest Father John Crean. In the early years of the take-over, he was helped by Père Jean-Marie Chuffart who later became Superior at St. Thomas'.

Of the three churches in the Parish, St. Joseph's was the only one to disappear. In 1996, due to economical pressure on the Church, it was closed down, the last Mass held there on April 24th of that year. It was demolished, and the area turned into a housing estate.

St. Thomas' Parish

Ever since the re-integration of the Catholic churches in Jersey, it had been linguistic demarcations which had separated the French and Anglo-Irish communities. Even a regulation set up in March 1883 by Mgr John Virtue, Bishop of Portsmouth, regarding the two St. Helier Catholic Parishes, had its bases in essential linguistic differences, setting aside St. Mary and St. Peter for the Anglo-Irish and St. Thomas' for the French. In 1946, a report from St. Thomas' underlined the fact that Jersey's population was becoming less and less Francophone:

> It is a fact that since the 1914-18 War, not only the population of French origin but even the French-speaking one is largely diminishing. There are few children and young people able to speak or even understand French. For the good of our parishes we will have to make extensive use of the English language for Catechism, confessions and even preaching. As for Catechism, only two of us are able to teach it in English.[2]

At that time there were twelve French Oblates in Jersey and the two

Easter Decorations 1966, St. Thomas' Church
(Courtesy of Bernard Holley)

English-speaking ones were Père Choinel and Jersey-born Père Durand. As the years progressed and the Anglo-Irish Province began to take over the former French Parishes, it was clear that the only French Parish to remain active in the Island would ultimately be in St. Helier – ie: St. Thomas'. By the 1960s the number of French Oblates in Jersey was decreasing whilst the number of Anglo-Irish priests was on the rise. The Anglo-Irish were still able to afford changes and developments to their establishments, whilst the French community was under constant financial pressure, needing the linguistic support of the Anglophone clerics to continue working in Jersey. St. Thomas' Parish was the last remaining French stronghold in the Island, the church still regarded by many churchgoers as the French Cathedral.

Additionally, fewer people were attending Mass, and fewer were devoting their time to Church activities. This applied to both the French and the Anglo-Irish groups. Already in the late 1960s, the annual Corpus Christi parades through the streets of St. Helier ceased to take place, the official reason being that the town's increased traffic would not tolerate the pressure of the thousands who thronged through the streets. In 1971, when the *Suisse*, Mr. Ferdinand Lecrivain, died, nobody replaced his role, and there has been no *Suisse* at St. Thomas' Church since then. An old tradition was gone.

The 1980s were perhaps the final turning point as far as the survival of a French Oblate community in Jersey was concerned; and the irony of this lies in the fact that many Jersey people believe it was an indirect result of the consequences – or interpretations – of the Second Vatican Council which led to the final decline of the French presence in St. Thomas' Parish.

The Second Vatican Council, popularly called Vatican II, was convened by Pope John XXIII and it was concluded under Paul VI after the former's death. It took place between 1962 and 1965. Its announced purpose was the spiritual renewal of the Church and the reconsideration of its position in the modern world. The most spectacular innovation of the Council was the invitation extended to Protestant and Orthodox Eastern Churches to send observers; the meetings were attended by representatives from these denominations. The essence of the Council was to redesign the Church both physically and spiritually in such a way that people actually felt a much stronger affinity and warmth with their faith.

One of the announced aims of the conference was to consider reform of the liturgy, primarily to bring the layman into closer participation in the church services and therefore to encourage some diversity in language and practice. From the beginning, great emphasis was also laid upon the pastoral duties of the bishops, as distinguished from administrative duties. The effects of Vatican II were to "modernise" the Church in accordance with the times, and in order to achieve the desired active participation of the congregation, it was made clear that the use of the vernacular – or native language – would greatly benefit the worshippers whose knowledge of Latin may well be restricted. It was also implied that by changing the position of the altar and having the priest face the congregation instead of away from the people, the worshippers would be able to feel closer to the meaning of the Mass and therefore benefit from the stronger communion with God. Catholic churches throughout the world consequently made changes in accordance with the new guidelines – altars redesigned, new Mass procedures implemented, the use of Latin abandoned; and whilst millions will agree that their own parishes have adhered to the teachings of the Council and that these teachings have benefited the Church in general, others still argue that the interpretations of the messages given during the Second Vatican Council have been taken too literally and radically in some cases; there are many who feel that reactions to the Council were too abrupt, lacking the subtlety of progressive change or continuity with the past. It is not the purpose of this book to analyse the teachings of the Council or its implementation in churches; we shall merely take a look at how the interpretations of Vatican II affected the Catholic Church in Jersey.

As the early years of the 1980s unfolded, the two major Catholic churches of St. Helier underwent radical changes. In St. Thomas' Parish, it was decided to completely refurbish St. Thomas' Church. In St. Mary's and St. Peter's Parish, it became clear that the current church at Vauxhall, opened on August 8th 1867,[3] and needing a vast amount of financial resources to maintain the ever-increasing costs of repair required to the building, would have to be replaced by a more modern church. These decisions took place in the early eighties and plans were made with the architect William Davies to build a new church in the lower car park of Beaulieu School, incorporating elements of the old building's heritage within a highly modern architectural framework. It was, as the then head of the Roman Catholic Church in Jersey, Father David Mahy, remarked, a desire to underline continuity: "We would like people to feel that although it's a new building, it's not a new church."[4] The theme of continuity was the key to the success of the new church in Wellington Road which was consecrated on September 28th 1985. Although it incorporated all the new guidelines expressed in Vatican II, the very fact that this took place in an extremely contemporary building which did retain vestiges from the past, allowed the element of change to be accepted by the parishioners. The modern architecture allowed the element of innovation to be embraced even by those who were of a more traditional school. Most of the people I interviewed for the purpose of this survey claimed that even though it was a sad event to see the old Vauxhall Church demolished,[5] the actual transfer from Vauxhall to Wellington Road was well-orchestrated.

The same cannot be said of the changes at St. Thomas'. In 1982, the Rector of the Parish, Père Jean-Marie Chuffart, sent his parishioners a lengthy 1200-word letter in English informing them of the forthcoming changes at the church:

> The plan for the interior has been made by our architect, Mr. Bruno Isnard, from Paris, according to the regulations set by the Pope and the Council of Vatican II for the liturgy of the sacraments.
>
> The emphasis is put on the main altar which will be situated at the centre of the cross formed by the nave and the two transepts. It will be in white stone and will be placed on a new platform.[6]

This paragraph did not worry the parishioners who knew that changes to the position of the altar reflected one of the desires propounded in Vatican II. However, the move towards absolute minimalism and the radical re-arranging of the pews in the church **did** disturb many parishioners; and my own survey revealed that the majority of churchgoers were alarmed and dismayed by the following sections of Père Chuffart's letter:

> The Centre nave will be reserved for the congregation in order to give as many people as possible the chance to see the altar and to feel more the togetherness of God's family.

Our Bishop, who has approved our plan and expressed his appreciation of it, is particularly in favour of the centre nave to be used in its fullness by the congregation.

Two large aisles on each side of the columns will be used for the processions and for all our movements up and down the church.

Moreover, the moving of the pews for the seating in the centre nave will have another interesting result for us and the people who will visit our church.

As it is at the moment, the fact that parts of the main pillars are hidden by the pews does not give full credit to the beauty of our church. When you look at these pillars, when the church is empty, it seems that these columns are cut by the benches at three feet above their real base or that they are resting on the pews.

The beauty of a gothic church is fully apparent when you can see the columns coming up from the ground and joining at the top, it is in fact what gives that peaceful and dignified atmosphere to a church like ours. Therefore, by having the benches detached from the columns, we shall gain a better view of the whole church.[7]

The letter concludes with the following wording:

Of course we, your priests, realise that this brings a noticeable change in our church and that changes are sometimes hard to accept, but we will ask of you an act of trust in the new plan as we feel quite sure that we will all be very pleased with the beauty of the final result.[8]

The letter is signed by Père Chuffart "on behalf of your priests, Père C. Morel and Père V. Igoa". Many felt that Père Chuffart was blinded in his desire to carry out the teachings of Vatican II, and in so doing, made some grave mistakes when refurbishing St. Thomas' Church. The plans outlined in the letter were duly carried out, and on Good Friday in 1983 at the opening of the new church interior, the central aisle had gone completely and was replaced by blocks of pews. Many of the old artifacts had likewise been stripped from the church including the old pulpit, and the walls were now bereft of the religious murals which had been a part of the church for so many years. In fact, minimalism was the order of the day. Very few of the parishioners spoken to for the purpose of my survey said they were satisfied with this new look for their *Cathédrale*, and many feel that the whole purpose of Vatican II was distorted by the new redesigning of their church. Some suggested that it led to fewer parishioners actually attending Mass at St. Thomas' after the refurbishment, and that, coupled with the linguistic and demographic changes in Jersey, it inevitably led to the departure of the French Oblates and a need for change.

Interior of St. Thomas' Church in 1983 (Courtesy of St. Thomas' Church)

The fact that the new Mass abandoned Latin in favour of the vernacular also begged the obvious question: what **was** Jersey's vernacular in the latter half of the twentieth century? It was certainly not French. It was English. As for a secondary language, Portuguese was becoming a far more prominent language in the Island than French. In fact, there were very few French-speakers left in the Island. Only a minimum number of Masses were now held in French, and by the mid-1990s it became clear to the French Oblates that they would no longer be needed in Jersey. Père Vincent Igoa, who jokingly referred to himself as "the last of the Mohicans"[9] was the last French Oblate priest in Jersey, and on September 6th 1999, a significant date in the history of St. Thomas' Church, Père Igoa left St. Thomas'. A huge chapter in Jersey's Catholic Church history was over.

St. Thomas' Church restored in 2007

Conclusion

The gradual decline of the French Catholic Church in Jersey since the end of World War II marked the end of an era which many of those I interviewed for the purpose of this book remember with fondness, joy and warmth. It is the warmth of this age now gone which I have hopefully brought to life in this book.

The past will not be forgotten. Woven into the fabric of buildings, images and memories, its spirit hovers over the entire Island. And as one homes in on St. Thomas' Church, splendidly refurbished in 2006-2007 under the direction of Canon Nicholas France, the legacy of the Oblate priests who built it and served in it seems to radiate through every window.

As one admires the beauty of the French Cathedral and walks down the newly-restored centre aisle, the church becomes filled with the voices of priests and nuns, men, women and children, a choir of French and Latin. May the voices of our past illuminate our future. *Deo Gratias*.

Notes

Introduction
[1] Balleine, G.R., *History of Jersey, Revised and Enlarged by Marguerite Syvret and Joan Stevens,* Phillimore, 1998, 2001 (hereafter referred to as Balleine)

Chapter 1
1 The *Ancien Régime* ("Old Order") refers primarily to the aristocratic, social and political system established in France under the Valois and Bourbon dynasties. France was an absolute monarchy.
[2] Some historians refer to the *Etats* as Estates. As this work is directly linked to Jersey's history, and our own Island background can refer to the notion of the three historical States, I feel this term has more relevance.
[3] Denis Diderot (1713-1784) was a prominent figure in the Enlightenment, and was the editor-in-chief of the famous *Encyclopédie*. His philosophy challenged set ideas and conventions, and he had a great belief in the importance of free will.
[4] François Marie Arouet de Voltaire (1694-1778), whose philosophy was based on scepticism and rationalism, influenced greatly the popularisation of science during his lifetime. Although his desire for reform may have fuelled some of the unrest leading up to the French Revolution, he had a horror of the potential fanaticism of people and the violence of revolution. Some of his writings were banned in France.
[5] Jean-Jacques Rousseau (1712-1778) was one of the most influential thinkers during the Enlightenment in eighteenth century Europe. His *Social Contract* of 1762 was banned by the French authorities.
[6] *The Declaration of the Rights of Man and Citizen* – proclaimed on August 26th 1789.
[7] *Constitution civile du clergé* – hereafter referred to as the *Civil Constitution of the Clergy* was passed on July 12, 1790 during the French Revolution, and subordinated the Roman Catholic Church in France to the French government.
[8] The new calendar was used by the French government for about 12 years from late 1793.
[9] In 1779 an expedition under the command of the Prince of Nassau attempted an unsuccessful landing in St. Ouen's Bay. In 1781, the French made another attempt to capture Jersey, this attempt culminating in the Battle of Jersey.
[10] The name Magot is derived from the French word meaning cheese-mite. This name was given to them contemptuously by Charlot followers, and the Jeannots defiantly adopted it.
[11] The *Gazette*'s issue of October 13th 1792 printed a very strong pro-Jacobin political statement.
[12] Baron E. de Demuin, *Histoire Religieuse de l'Ile de Jersey,* Rennes 1893.
[13] *Gazette de l'Ile de Jersey,* April 9th 1791.
[14] Isherwood, F.P. (ed.), *Banished by the Revolution, Jersey Catholic Record,* 1972, pp.114-115.

[15] Reproduced and translated *in Jersey Church History*, Vol 5, 1974 (hereafter referred to as *JCH*).

[16] François-René de Chateaubriand (1768-1848) was born in St. Malo and is considered to be the founder of French Romanticism.

[17] François-René de Chateaubriand, *Mémoires d'outre-tombe*, Book X, Chap 3, Sec 2.

[18] 1858-1946. Commonly known as Estourbeillon, he was a militant Breton politician and historian who was awarded both the Palmes Académiques and La Légion d'Honneur for his work. His major work regarding Jersey's French *émigrés* is the monumental 680-page *Les familles françaises à Jersey pendant la Révolution*, Nantes, 1886.

[19] One of the Abbé Amédée Guillotin de Corson (1837-1905)'s most significant works with direct links to Jersey is his *Les confesseurs de la Foi pendant la Grande Révolution sur le territoire de l' archidiocèse de Rennes*, Rennes, 1900.

[20] F.P. Isherwood translated large chunks of Demuin's work and published his research in numerous issues of the *Jersey Catholic Record*.

[21] Joseph Toussaint, *La déportation du clergé de Coutances et Avranches à la Révolution*, Avranches, 1979.

[22] According the Bill, no Catholic taking the Oath was henceforward to be prosecuted for being a Papist, for being educated in the Catholic religion, for hearing Mass or saying it, for being a priest or deacon, for entering into, or belonging to, any ecclesiastical order or community in the Church of Rome, or for assisting at, or performing any Catholic rites or ceremonies.

[23] Jean Calvin (1509-1564), Protestant reformer and theologian.

[24] An example of this attitude is apparent throughout the book by Charles Le Quesne entitled *A Constitutional History of Jersey*, published in London in 1856.

[25] When Southwark was divided by the Letters Apostolic of Pope Leo XIII in 1882, the new Diocese of Portsmouth took over.

[26] This in fact applied until 1842.

[27] *JCH*, Vol 5, p.9.

[28] There has been some debate as to his precise date of birth and forenames. According to the research by Walter J. Le Quesne and Guy Dixon, Matthieu de Gruchy was baptized on August 4th 1761 and did not have the middle name Francis as is suggested by other sources. Le Quesne and Dixon, *The de Gruchys of Jersey*, Jersey, 1991 & 2000, pp.30-32.

[29] L'Abbé du Tressay, *Vie de Matthieu de Gruchy*, Paris, 1868.

[30] The Parish Church of Saint-Mars-La-Réorthe houses a stained-glass window by Roger Degas depicting his execution, and other villages of the area have streets or squares named after the Jerseyman.

[31] Tina Spencer-Nairn, *Matthew Francis de Gruchy – A Brief History to Commemorate the 200th Anniversary of his Death*, St. Matthew's Parish, 1997.

[32] The Church at Beauvoir-sur-Mer contains a stained-glass window depicting Matthieu de Gruchy on his way to his execution.

[33] Balleine, p223.

[34] *JCH*, Vol 1, 1971, p19.

[35] His grave's disappearance from the cemetery was investigated in full by Jean Nicholas René de la Croix, and is explained in detail in his book *Jersey, ses Antiquités, ses Institutions, son Histoire*, 3 vol., Jersey, 1859-1861.

[36] Père de Grimouville opted to look after the Catholic soldiers and Irish workers in the Island.

Chapter 2

[1] *JCH*, Vol 6, p.5.

[2] One famous outburst against the Catholic Church was in April 1853 at Macpéla Cemetery, the most common burial place for the political exiles (or *proscrits*) who had fled to Jersey following the 1848 *coup d'état*. Another anti-clerical demonstration took place a few days earlier, this time at Green Street Cemetery, where red flags were carried with no priest present. Related in the comprehensive study by Philip Stevens, *Victor Hugo in Jersey*, London, 1985 (2002), pp.69-70.

[3] *Ibid.*, p.36.

[4] Père Jean François Volkeryck (1828-1906). Various spellings of his name appear in different reference works, Volkerick and Volkerijk being the most common. I have opted for the version verified in Lokeren, Belgium, where he is buried.

[5] *Les Religieuses de Saint-André*, Lille, Paris, Tournay, Bruges, 1908, p.149. Hereafter referred to as *LRSA*.

[6] In Britain, the Sisters are often referred to as the St. Andrew's Sisters; however, most references to the Order in Jersey retain their French name.

[7] *LRSA*, p.151.

[8] *Ibid.*, p.152.

[9] *Ibid.*, p.153.

[10] Brother Edward was the founding headmaster of the new De La Salle College in 1917. His Diary was translated into English by Brother Lawrence Anthony.

[11] *De La Salle Golden Jubilee 1917-1867*, Jersey, 1967, p.35.

[12] *LDSA*, p.208-209.

[13] Alfred-Louis Frangeul (1833-1905) came from a family of architects. His work in Brittany included restoring St. Malo Cathedral and building churches in Cancale, Plancoët and Pleurtuit. Between 1863 and 1878 he was Chief Architect of St. Malo.

[14] The De La Salle Brothers then moved into Albion House where they stayed until 1884.

[15] Vincent Igoa O.M.I., *A Hundred Years of Life in Jersey*, Jersey, 1981, p.9.

[16] *LRSA* p. 237.

[17] September 4th 1870 marked the capitulation of Napoleon III and the birth of the Third Republic in France.

[18] *LRSA*, p.237.

[19] The stained glass windows in the church were created in 1927-28 by Joseph Benoit (1871-1936) whose work was in constant demand in Nancy in north-eastern France.

Chapter 3

[1] As more religious orders settled into this part of town, the whole of the Wellington Road / St. Saviour's Road hillside commonly became known as Holy Hill.

[2] The land on which Beaulieu House was built in 1825 was purchased by François Bertram on November 13th 1824. On his death in 1873, the house and accompanying land were passed on to his grandson whose widow sold the property to the *Auxiliatrices*.

[3] The English novices were sent to London that same year to form the English Novitiate.

[4] Also known as Didron the Younger, to distinguish him from Adolphe-Napoléon Didron (the Elder: 1806-1867), the Parisian archeologist and art historian who also worked on the restoration and design of stained glass windows in France, including one window at Notre-Dame de Paris.

[5] One window specifically refers to the Jesuit motto AMDG: Ad Majorem Dei Gloriam

(For the Greater Glory of God). Two windows depict scenes from Purgatory with the inclusion of flames amidst religious scenes.

[6] Bishop Augustin René Louis Le Mintier, the last Bishop of Tréguier, fled to Jersey in 1791. He died in London in 1801 and was later interred in Tréguier Cathedral.

[7] Furthermore, as we shall discover later, this was not the first sculpture by Hernot II in Jersey with strong Catholic connections.

[8] They remained at Beaulieu until 1950. After having suffered great deprivation during the Second World War, they realised that the German Occupation had curtailed their work considerably; funding was low and their need to leave Jersey became apparent.

[9] The original plot of land was known as La Frégonnière, and consisted of two farm buildings with a large orchard extending to the top of the hill. The Imperial Hotel was built on this land in 1866.

[10] *JCH*, Vol 7, p.3.

[11] *Ibid.*, p.4.

[12] *Ibid.*, p.4.

[13] Eileen Nicolle, *A History of Highlands College*, Jersey, 2000, p.10.

[14] *JCR*, January 1972, p.12.

[15] *JCH*, Vol 7, p.12.

[16] *Ibid.*, p.13.

[17] Théophile Seyrig (1843-1923) is famed for his metal bridges and viaducts including the Dom Luís Bridge over the Douro in Portugal.

[18] *Jersey Express*, October 23rd 1894.

Chapter 4

[1] The motto of the Oblates – "He sent me to Evangelise the Poor".

[2] On May 19th 1882, due to a change within the Episcopal system in England, the Channel Islands now came under the jurisdiction of the newly-created Diocese of Portsmouth which had branched away from Southwark. Mgr. John Virtue (1826-1900) was the first Bishop of the Diocese of Portsmouth, ordained on July 25th 1882.

[3] *LRSA*, p.239.

[4] *LRSA*, pp. 241-242.

[5] *Ibid*, p. 242.

[6] *Ibid*, p.243.

[7] *Ibid*, pp.243-244.

[8] The Immaculate Conception was defined as a dogma by Pope Pius IX in 1854. This was not any specific insignia referring to the *Dames de Saint-André*, but was a common tribute to the Virgin Mary. It also blended in harmoniously with the full title of the Oblates of Mary Immaculate.

[9] *Souvenir du Centenaire de la Congrégation des Missionnaires Oblats de Marie Immaculée 1816-1916*, (published at St. Mary's House - Sacré Cœur Orphanage), 1916, p.35. (hereafter referred to as *Souvenir*).

[10] An earlier attempt to open a school and chapel in St. Ouen was made in 1873 before the arrival of the Oblates, an initiative undertaken by Père Basté, Curate at St. Thomas'. With no resident preist at St. Matthew's the venture was unsuccessful.

[11] In 1929 the bell was replaced by three new bells and was later transferred to St. Anne's Church in St. Ouen. In 1989 it was re-erected at St. Matthew's in the garden of the presbytery in memory of the Oblate Fathers.

[12] The house was named after Charles-Ferdinand de Bourbon, Duc de Berry (1778-1820) who built it in 1814 whilst exiled in Jersey. His stay is charted in detail by

François-René Chateaubriand who knew Jersey from his own period of exile in the Island during the French Revolution. The Duke was murdered in Paris by Pierre-Louis Louvel on February 14th 1820. Berry House was demolished in 1975, although it is known that Père Jean-Marie Chuffart had sought permission to redevelop the property in 1972.

[13] Laurent-Achille Rey O.M.I. (1828-1911) had earlier been the first Chaplain to serve the original Sacré Cœur Chapel at Montmartre in 1876, erected as a temporary place of worship whilst the actual Basilica was being built.

[14] Both Père Guiramand and Père Tardivon are buried at the church, Père Tardivon's grave situated by the sacristy wall.

[15] *LRSA*, p.251.

[16] *Souvenir*, p.39.

[17] *LRSA*, pp. 251-252.

[18] *Ibid*, p.232.

[19] Vincent Igoa, *A Hundred Years of Life in Jersey*, Jersey, 1981, p.10.

[20] Unpublished Oblate notes.

[21] J.L. Messager, *The Story and Description of St. Thomas' Catholic Church, St. Helier, Jersey, Channel Islands*, Liverpool, 1961, p.3.

[22] *JCH*, Vol 6, 1974, p. 3.

[23] *Ibid*, p.3.

[24] *Ibid*, p.3.

[25] *Ibid*, p.3

[26] *LRSA*, p.244.

[27] Jean-Marie Huchet (1841-1914) was one of the most prominent late 19th Century building contractors Pèreom Rennes'; this was not his first collaboration with the architect Afred Louis Frangeul.

[28] "It seems likely that advantage was taken of the new railway extension to La Moye Quarry that was opened on 30th August 1884." D. Tipping, *La Cathédral (sic)*, (private publication) Jersey, 2006, p.11.

[29] Laurent-Charles Maréchal (1801-1887) was one of France's leading glass artists; amongst his most famous pieces is a window at the castle of Fontainebleau.

[30] Georges-Claudius Lavergne (1814-1887).

[31] The Little Sisters of the Poor (Jeanne Jugan residence) is still situated on the original site but the property underwent considerable re-modernisation during the 1970s, and all but the Chapel was demolished in order to build the current premises. The foundation stone for the new development was laid by Bishop Worlock of Portsmouth on September 10th 1972.

[32] The house was expanded in 1908, and after Mère Marie Madeleine became Superior in 1909, an operating theatre was added. Another new wing was added in 1936. As from 1970 the house reverted to being a nursing home, and in 1991 the old building was demolished to build a new residential home.

Chapter 5

[1] The school building was known as the Thomas Julian Bray Jubilee Hall for many years, also as the Sacré Cœur School. It is on the site of the current St. Julian's Hall Apartments.

[2] *L'Echo de Saint-Hélier*, May 1901, p.28.

[3] *Ibid*, pp.27-28.

[4] This boys' school was staffed by the Brothers of Christian Instruction of Ploërmel.

-Léon-Joseph Legrand was born in La Gorgne on November 8th 1854 and died in Jersey on September 18th 1940. He is buried at Almorah Cemetery.

[6] Emile Combes (1835-1921) was President of the Council between 1902 and 1905 and was the driving force of the separation of Church and State.

[7] On December 9th 1905, a law was passed in France separating the Church and the State. This law was based on three principles: the neutrality of the state, the freedom of exercise of religion, and public powers related to the church. This law is seen as the backbone of the French principle of *laïcité*. The law famously states "The Republic neither recognises, nor salaries, nor subsidises any religion."

[8] *L'Echo de Saint-Hélier*, May 1901, p.27.

[9] *Ibid*, August 1901, p.53.

[10] *Ibid*, December 1902, p.93.

[11] Between 1884 and 1896 he was Superior at a seminary in Heer near Maastricht which had an overwhelming number of German students. Père Legrand could speak fluent German.

[12] Author's interview with Jean "Jack" Jouanny on January 4th 2007.

[13] *Personal View/Interviews of Islanders*, Jersey Archive.

[14] *Ibid*.

[15] The famous bell foundry Paccard of Annecy was founded in 1796 by Antoine Paccard.

[16] According to J.L. Messager, the organ was fully reconditioned in 1959 by the pipe organ builders Henry Willis & Sons of Liverpool. J.L. Messager, *The Story and Description of St. Thomas' Catholic Church*, p.6.

[17] The ancient bell foundry of Cornille-Havard is situated in Villedieu-les-Poêles in Normandy.

[18] The uniforms are on loan to St. Thomas' Church.

[19] *Jersey Morning News*, June 23rd 1930.

[20] *Ibid*.

[21] *Ibid*.

[22] *Jersey Critic*, June 13th 1931.

[23] Vincent Igoa, *A Hundred Years of Life in Jersey*, p. 18.

[24] In 1938 it became the Playhouse Theatre.

[25] Vincent Igoa, *A Hundred Years of Life in Jersey*, p. 36.

[26] Apart from 1941-47 for which there are no diary entries whatsoever.

[27] *Codex Historicus* by Oblate Rectors of St. Matthew's, p.10 (hereafter referred to as *Codex*).

[28] *Ibid*, p.138.

[29] Town in the Diocese of Laval where it is believed the Virgin Mary made an appearance in 1871. The town also housed the new Oblate seminary, opened after St. Joseph's College in Jersey closed in 1931.

[30] *Codex*, p.138.

Chapter 6

[1] Pauline Reynolds became known as Sister Thérèse de Jésus. Her life is charted in the work by P. Picot, *Pauline Reynolds, Anglaise convertie – Religieuse Carmélite au Monastère du Saint-Enfant-Jésus de Saint-Pair (Manche)*, Paris, 1915.

[2] *Ibid*, p.206.

[3] *Ibid*, p.207.

[4] *Ibid*, p.211.

[5] *Ibid*, p.212.

[6] Unpublished letter from the Archives of the Carmel de Saint-Pair.

[7] All four properties – Goodlands, Westbourne Terrace, Ker Anna and Hautmont – are still standing, although the Goodlands estate has been separated into individual dwellings.

[8] Eighteen Carmelite sisters from the St. Brieuc Carmel died in Jersey, and their remains are now at Almorah Cemetery.

[9] George W. Croad, *A Jersey Album*, Jersey, 1981, pp.145-146.

[10] Eileen Nicolle, *A History of Highlands College*, p.19.

[11] The eight boys who drowned were Antoine Elie de Beaumont, Christian Beaufils, Marie-Jacques des Gachons, Alain de Kerros, René Kerdal, Alfred Marchand, Jean Freed and his brother Emmanuel. The entire story of the tragedy can be read in the volume *En Souvenir du 7 juillet 1915*, Bigwood, Jersey.

[12] http://www.teilhard.org.uk/frameset.asp

[13] *JCR*, May 1972, p.6.

[14] In 1908 the Council acquired premises at Ashton House, 113 Rouge Bouillon.

[15] St. Mary's College is an active Roman Catholic school and still promotes the motto and religious teaching of Jean-Marie de Lammenais.

[16] This building now houses the Education Committee. The statue of St. Joseph still dominates the entrance.

[17] *L'Echo des Missions des Frères de l'Instruction Chrétienne*, November 1922, p.102.

[18] Familiar French for a tin hut.

[19] The Brothers would hold a major annual spiritual retreat in early August.

[20] *JCR*, May 1972, p.9.

[21] Père Christian Burdo (1881-1961) was also a close friend of Pierre Teilhard de Chardin; they first met when studying in Jersey and later at Ore Place, Hastings. Père Burdo later took part in a number of significant archaeological digs in Jersey, and played a major role in the excavations at Pinnacle Rock between 1930 and 1935.

[22] *JCH*, Vol 7, pp.10-11.

[23] *Jersey Morning News*, January 28th 1929.

[24] *Jersey Evening Post*, February 20th 1929.

[25] He died in France in March 1981 after a leg fracture in 1979 forced him to retire. Both Père Rey and Pierre Teilhard de Chardin are featured on a 1982 Jersey stamp series entitled Links with France.

[26] The centre of the Internation Union of World Geophysics.

[27] The De La Salle Brothers had been at Les Vauxbelets in Guernsey since 1904.

[28] Of the Sangan family who now operated the Summerland Knitwear Factory at Rouge Bouillon.

[29] *Jersey Morning News*, September 12th 1918.

[30] This took place in 1954.

Chapter 7

[1] One such attempt was made in 1900 when it was suggested the schools did not reach the required standards; however, this mini-crisis reached a positive conclusion for the Catholics in March 1901 when Her Majesty's Inspector certified that all the Catholic schools in the Island satisfied his requirements.

[2] *JCH*, Vol 6, 1974, p.17.

[3] Marie Madeleine Victoire de Bengy, Vicomtesse de Bonnault d'Houet, was born in 1781 and died in 1858. It is understood she visited Jersey briefly in 1831 on her way

back to France from London.

[4] *Formation, Instruction, Affection – Sisters Faithful Companions of Jesus in Jersey – 1911-2002*, Manchester, 2002, p. 8. (Hereafter referred to as *FIA*).

[5] *Ibid*, p.9.

[6] This property later became the Palace Hotel and was blown up by mutinous German soldiers in March 1945.

[7] *FIA*, p.11.

[8] *Ibid*, pp.19-20.

[9] *Ibid*, p.15.

[10] *Codex*, p.4.

[11] *Ibid*, p.7.

[12] *Ibid*, p.8.

[13] Amongst Julien Barbier's achievements are the Parish Church of Cachan, the chapel at Châlo Saint-Mars and the Eglise Sacré Cœur in Dijon.

[14] *FIA*, p.22.

[15] On June 1st 1925 St. Aubin's once more reverted to being part of St. Thomas' Parish.

[16] In 1931 Council 238 of the Knights of St. Columba was set up in St. Martin; they also contributed greatly to modernising the former school which soon became known as Columba Hall.

[17] On November 16th 1924, the day before his wedding, he was presented with a clock by the Parish of St. Matthew to thank him for all his years of service to the chapel.

[18] Charles Desvergnes (1860-1928) was born in Bellegarde and studied at l'Ecole Nationale des Beaux-Arts. He was awarded the Grand Prix de Rome in 1889, and soon became famous in Paris for his statues of Joan of Arc.

[19] *Codex*, p.18.

[20] *Ibid*, p.19.

[21] Amongst the Congregations contacted, it is known that the *Filles du Saint-Esprit de St. Brieuc* were approached directly, however the price-tag on the property was far too high for them.

[22] The De La Salle Brothers had agreed to let the FCJ Sisters keep the statues until they left the Convent; however, the Sisters insisted on the Brothers taking the statues at once.

[23] *Codex*, p. 20.

[24] Unpublished letter from Mgr Cotter to Père Pitard, September 27th 1923.

[25] *Jersey Evening Post*, October 3rd 1923.

[26] *Jersey Critic*, October 1923.

[27] *Codex*, p.22.

[28] *Codex*, p.37.

[29] She died in 1874.

[30] By then, this district was under the supervision of the Anglo-Irish Oblates of St. Aubin.

[31] *Notice nécrologique sur le R.P. Alain Mao, O.M.I. par le R.P. Lemius, O.M.I., Ancien Supérieur de Montmartre*, St. Thomas' Church Archives.

Chapter 8

[1] Author's own survey.

[2] *FIA*, pp.23-26.

[3] *Ibid*, p.26.

[4] *Ibid*, pp.26-27.

[5] Numbers of pupils did rise again after the first year of Occupation.

[6] *De La Salle College Golden Jubilee 1917-1967*, Loughborough, 1967, p.49.

[7] *Chronique des Frères de L'Instruction Chrétienne de Ploërmel*, July 1946, pp.73-74. (Hereafter referred to as *CFICP*).

[8] This Order was founded in Broons in 1828 by two sisters, Louise and Laurence Lemarchand. The motherhouse and convent are still situated in Broons. The Sisters based at Highlands stayed in the Island until 1954.

[9] *CFICP*, November 1946, p.79.

[10] *Ibid*, March 1947, p. 218.

[11] Père Jaïn returned to Jersey after the War and became a curate at St. Thomas'. He also became the Hospital Chaplain. He died in 1974 in his 77th year.

[12] The new church of St. Patrick's was built after the War and was opened on March 20th 1949.

[13] Père Choinel is fondly remembered by many Islanders who recall the episode after the War when he reversed his car into the harbour when picking up priests who had arrived by boat from France. Thankfully nobody was injured.

[14] This story was originally researched by Len Stevens for the October 1971 issue of the *Jersey Catholic Record*.

[15] *Jersey Weekly Post*, October 6th 1945.

[16] *JCR*, Feb-March, 1974, p.22. Père Durand died on November 6th 1973.

[17] *Les Chroniques de Jersey*, August 25th 1945.

[18] It is of interest to note that amongst the hundreds of mourners who attended the Requiem Mass were artists Lucy Schwob and her stepsister Suzanne Malherbe (also known as Claude Cahun and Marcel Moore). They had been sentenced to death by the Germans for their Resistance work, but were reprieved.

Chapter 9

[1] In 1937 Vauxhall Elementary School, which had been governed by the States of Jersey, was re-opened by the FCJs as a free private elementary school to secure the teaching of religion.

[2] *FIA*, p.22.

[3] André Ferrari, *Jersey's Lost Heritage – Fifty Years of Needless Destruction*, Jersey, 1996, p.52.

[4] *Ibid*, p.54.

[5] *FIA*, p.44.

[6] *Ibid*, p.46.

[7] Web article by F. Le Blancq: http://www.jerseymet.gov.je/climate/louis.html

[8] Eileen Nicolle, *A History of Highlands College*, p.26.

[9] The initial discussions between the States of Jersey and the Ploërmel Brothers began in April 1971.

[10] *CFICP*, October 1972, p.317.

[11] Letter from Frère Joseph Pinel to Diane Moore, January 10th 2007.

[12] The main buildings including the former chapel and *Salle des Fêtes* have been preserved by the current owner Richard Brocken (Premier Shopfitting and Contracting Ltd).

Chapter 10

[1] Archbishop Augustin Dontenwill (1857-1931) was Superior General of the Oblates from 1908 until his death. He visited Jersey on a number of occasions.

[2] Vincent Igoa, *A Hundred Years of Life in Jersey*, pp. 41-45.

[3] There had been two churches at Vauxhall. The first was built in 1843. The second church was designed by Joseph Aloysius Hansom (1803-1882), the creator of the Hansom Cab.

[4] Julie A. Lush, *St. Mary's and St. Peter's Church*, Jersey, 1984, p.42.

[5] The final celebration of Mass at Vauxhall took place on August 29th 1984. The church was sold to the States of Jersey and demolished the year after.

[6] St. Thomas' Church Archives.

[7] *Ibid.*

[8] *Ibid.*

[9] Interview with the author.

Select Bibliography

Balleine, G.R., *History of Jersey*, Revised and Enlarged by Marguerite Syvret and Joan Stevens, Phillimore, 1998, 2001

Codex Historicus (unpublished Oblate Diary)

Croad, George W., *A Jersey Album*, Jersey, 1981

De La Salle Golden Jubilee 1917-1967, Jersey, 1967

Demuin, Baron E., *Histoire Religieuse de l'Ile de Jersey*, Rennes, 1893

Ferrari, André, *Jersey's Lost Heritage – Fifty Years of Needless Destruction*, Jersey, 1996

Formation, Instruction, Affection – Sisters Faithful Companions of Jesus in Jersey, 1911-2002, Jersey, 2002

Hamoniaux, F., *Souvenir du Centenaire de la Congrégation des Missionnaires Oblats de Marie Immaculée 1816-1916*, Jersey, 1916

Igoa, Vincent, *A Hundred Years of Life in Jersey*, 1880-1980 OMI, Jersey, 1981

Isherwood, F.P. (ed), *Banished by the Revolution*, Jersey Catholic Record, 1972

Isherwood, F.P. (ed), *Jersey Church History*, Vols I-VIII

Les Religieuses de Saint-André, Lille, Paris, Tournay, Bruges, 1908

Messager, J.L., *The Story and Description of St. Thomas' Catholic Church, St. Helier, Jersey, Channel Islands*, Liverpool, 1961

Nicolle, Eileen, *A History of Highlands College*, Jersey, 2000

Picot, P., *Pauline Reynolds, Anglaise convertie – Religieuse Carmélite au*

Monastère du Saint Enfant-Jésus de Saint-Pair (Manche), Paris, 1915

Tressay, L'Abbé du, *Vie de Matthieu de Gruchy*, Paris, 1868

Newspapers and Periodicals

Chronique des Frères de l'Instruction Chrétienne de Ploërmel

De Mazenod Record

Gazette de l'Ile de Jersey

L'Echo des Missions des Frères de l'Instruction Chrétienne

L'Echo de Saint-Hélier

Jersey Catholic Record

Jersey Critic

Jersey Express

Jersey Morning News

Jersey Evening Post

Missions de la Congrégation des Oblats

Unless otherwise stated or credited, all photography as well as translations from French into English are by Diane Moore.

The Author

Diane Moore was born in Jersey. She studied Modern Languages and Literature at the universities of London (King's College), Freiburg, Geneva, Exeter and Oslo. She also studied theology (AKC) at King's College London. Diane's previous publications include poetry, drama and literary criticism.

Index